A Roller-coaster Ride
Thoughts on aging

Books by Naomi Beth Wakan

Book Ends: A year between the covers
Compositions: Notes on the written word
Haiku: One Breath Poetry
Late Bloomer: On Writing Later in Life
Segues

A Roller-coaster Ride
Thoughts on aging

Naomi Beth Wakan

POPLAR
PRESS

Published in Canada by Poplar Press, a division of Wolsak and Wynn
Publishers Ltd., Hamilton.

Cover image:
Cover design: Julie McNeill
Author's photograph: Eli Wakan
Typeset in Stone Serif
Printed by Ball Media, Brantford, Canada

The publisher gratefully acknowledges the support
of the Canada Council for the Arts, the Ontario
Arts Council and the Canada Book Fund.

The Canada Council | Le Conseil des Arts
for the Arts | du Canada

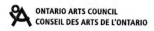

ONTARIO ARTS COUNCIL
CONSEIL DES ARTS DE L'ONTARIO

Poplar Press
#102 – 69 Hughson Street North
Hamilton, ON
Canada L8R 1G5

Canadian   Patrimoine
Heritage   canadien

Sections of this book were previously published in *Senior Living Magazine*
as "The Lovely Old Biddy," "Memories Through Poetry" and "My Robot
House."

The nostalgia tanka in "Looking Back" were reprinted from *Nostalgia and
the Attic*, with permission from my co-author, Alice Rich.

Library and Archives Canada Cataloguing in Publication
Wakan, Naomi
        A roller-coaster ride : thoughts on aging / Naomi Beth Wakan.

Includes bibliographical references.
ISBN 978-1-894987-64-6

        1. Aging--Social aspects. 2. Aging--Psychological aspects.
3. Wakan, Naomi. I. Title.

HQ1061.W34 2012   305.26   C2012-900480-4

To Eli, who promised, and kept his word,
to grow old along with me.

And to Dr. John Sloan, who still does house calls
and treats his fragile patients as individuals. If he
had ten thousand clones, the Canadian health care
system would be in much better shape.

Table of Contents

Introduction

Though I am in my eighties now, I do not seem to have moved into the calm and wisdom that people promised me old age would bring. My life is more like a roller coaster. Some days I feel totally part of the universe. Life seems interconnected and meaningful and the words flow from me as if coming from a deep source. Death slots in naturally as all things come into being and pass away. Other times everything falls to pieces. The world outside seems menacing and fearful and death a losing game. So fittingly, my publisher and I chose *A Roller-coaster Ride* as the title for this collection of essays and poetry on aging.

Writing around the topic of aging is bound to bring up memories and from moment to moment as I wrote the book, I have to confess I have been trapped in nostalgia for times of great happiness. But the traps didn't catch me for too long, for, ever practical, and a survivor by bloodline, the continual urge to create the most attractive present possible brought me back to my little cottage on Gabriola Island. One of the nostalgic memories was of my teen years in Blackpool, a honky-tonk-style town in Lancashire, to which our family had been evacuated during the war. It was a roller-coaster kind of town both literally and metaphorically, for it had a Golden Mile of sideshows, rides and roller coasters to amuse the day trippers to the seaside. In summer the town was a mess of folks from the mill towns, fish and chip papers, dirty postcards and Blackpool Rock – a candy cane with the word "Blackpool" miraculously written throughout the stick. In winter, the sandy beaches were bare of holidaymakers, of donkey rides, of everything. A solitary pair, such as my twin and I, could wander them at leisure, like two characters in a French movie.

I write about the small and personal. I am the sort of person Friedrich Nietzsche describes as one "who never penetrates into the depths of a problem, yet often notices things that the professional with his laborious poring over it never does." Or better yet, I am, like Geoff Dyer, "a literary and scholarly gatecrasher, turning up uninvited at an area of expertise, making myself at home." I have rarely seen death close-up, have never accompanied a person through the stages of dying, and hardly ever go to funerals or wakes. Neither can I write about the intensities of aging. I can, however, write about the small concerns of an eighty-year-old person – my fears, my pleasures... No big moral statements, no big dramas, just a lot of questions; questions that you might also be asking. So please join me on my journey into aging.

The Inner Me

My publisher wrote to me before my last book, *Book Ends: A year between the covers*, came out, to ask me whether I would mind being called that "lovely old biddy from Gabriola" on advertising copy. I said, "not at all, go right ahead." I love to let my publisher do what she wants as much as I can, for that allows me to argue over the odd comma I want inserted when I really want it. After the book was launched, a concerned friend wrote to me, "I want to suggest that you discard the 'old biddy' bit you have in your information material. It's self-denigrating, stereotyping, a kind of 'ageism,' and unworthy of your notions of self-esteem."

I wrote back explaining how that phrase had originated by telling her that I was having a printing job done in Nanaimo, the closest town on Vancouver Island to the small island of Gabriola, where I live. The printer couldn't offer perfect binding, so the job had to partially go down to Victoria. My printer sent an email accompanying the job, and, by mistake, the email got sent to me. It began, "I have this lovely old biddy from Gabriola..." I laughed out loud when I read it and thereafter repeated the story endlessly at my readings. It was always good for a laugh, and laughter is good.

I was not demeaning myself, because I have a very firm image of myself as a bright, enthusiastic, but rather flighty young woman. That image has kept me going all my life while I achieved a moderate degree of success in several areas. Particularly it has allowed me to recognize my limits, and to see what a clown I basically am, yet know at the same time what a wise clown I am also. This image has taken me cheerfully through menopause and successfully into old age. From outside, people see a slightly stooped elder person with grey, thinning hair. I see that too when I look in the mirror. Inside, however, I am this bouncing, precocious, imaginative kid, naive with the kind of naivety that paradoxically becomes a kind of street smarts.

That inner image is important, even if it is only partially correct, for that is the image that sustains us through the years of possible indignity and non-caring. I'll give you another example. I have a friend who was a cute child and a cute, precocious teenager. She kept this image of being beautiful and youthful with her even though she now is wrinkled and obviously old. Recently she was in a poor country and was riding a bicycle through an unknown part of town. A man leapt out and knocked her from her bicycle. Her first thought was "he is going to rape me." She curled up tight and scrunched her eyes. Nothing happened. When she opened her eyes she could see the man off and away on her bicycle. It was the bike he wanted, not her beautiful body. She yelled after him to no avail but, because she is young and beautiful inside, she could allow herself to laugh. Laughing at her own foolishness was not degrading to her, it was empowering. She is not going to give up the image of her inner self, it maintains her. She is, however, intelligent enough to know it doesn't match how she is viewed by others.

Recently, I emceed an evening for a group of campus radio folk. While preparing for the event, I supposed their average age would be twenty-one. I am eighty. I wondered how on earth I was going to say anything of relevance for their already over-sophisticated ears to take in. I don't have much energy for fretting, however, as my writing is demanding and I am also a housekeeper and garden-weeder and wife and mother and many other things that make more pressing demands on my energies. I decided to just be myself – the outer self would wear something simple and elegant, something Meryl Streep might wear to the Oscars when all the other actors look like streetwalkers. The inner self would be the usual gawky, awkward, disarmingly open person I basically am; amusing people by just telling the truth as I see it, and throwing remarks around regardless of total appropriateness, because I have never bothered much about being appropriate.

Aging cannot be avoided. You will become, whether you like it or not, pushed to the edge of the crowd, rather than being the centre of attention. Unless you are very wealthy, you will be slipped in as an afterthought, called in from a reserve list of substitutes, smiled at benignly when you offer an opinion. If your inner image is still running along with you, as your shadow accompanies you on your outer edge, you will float through it all, assured that you still have value, and presenting your duck's feathers for the water of old-age prejudices to merely run off. You're cute, you're intelligent, you're beautiful, you're wrong...but how right you really are.

Shoulder pads

I always wanted to be
a cool tall woman with
shoulder pads who spoke
little, but knew where
she was going, or even
a cool tall woman with
shoulder pads who
spoke a lot and gave
orders in all directions,
knowing one of them
would be where she was going.
Or a small quiet ruthless
woman, who held her cards
close to her chest and also
knew where she was going.
My breasts were too big
to hold anything close
to my chest, so I smothered
and mothered my way through
life with not the slightest
idea of where I was going.
Now the women and I,
shoulder pads or not, are
all drawing our pensions
and it doesn't seem to matter
a jot whether we knew, or didn't
know where we were going.

Where's My Chin?

The difficulty of growing old is that one doesn't know what to do, through want of experience, [and] helplessly watches the waves breaking and civilisation growing older at the same rate as oneself. In youth experience is unnecessary: in age we count on it and, generally speaking, only act successfully when it is to hand. Inverted adolescence. The decay of our powers more puzzling than their birth, because our consciousness was born with them, but here it lags behind, looking at the symptoms and unable to decide which is to be taken seriously. Apart from its discomfort, it's so baffling.

– E. M. Forster, *Commonplace Book*

I had no hot flashes at menopause; apart from the ceasing of my monthly flow of blood, I had no symptoms at all. One day I looked in the mirror and was surprised that my chin didn't seem to be as firmly defined as usual. That was that. I was growing old. Others too seem to have caught their first sight of their aging by a similar glance in a mirror. A friend reported to me, "I was at a postural reconstruction therapist. She works with the client naked and lying on the carpet. Beside me on the carpet was propped a large mirror. As she was working on me, I happened to glance in it. My God! My skin is sagging, I thought. I was fifty at the time."

When I asked my husband, Eli, of his first intimation of aging he said, succinct as always, "The first time I hurt and I hadn't caused it." The writer Shirley Langer told me,

> It was easy to say at fifty that ageing
> wouldn't bother me. I could still look in the
> mirror and see what people would call "an
> attractive woman." The hair thick, streaks
> of iron gray glinting amongst the chestnut.
> Eyes not bagged. Crow's feet still subtle.
> The line of the lips distinct, not pruning.
> No dewlap swaying under the chin. Bristle
> facial hair limited to a mere few on the upper
> lip, and one, always the same one, on the
> chin. Flesh everywhere holding firm, the
> belly following normal childbirth curves.
> Toenails as yet unthickened. Veins visible,
> but not raised and ropy. The upper body
> distinct from the lower, not yet telescoped
> downward, obliterating the waist. Still
> satisfied, I would chastise people who weren't
> growing old gracefully. Now, at sixty three,
> I feel different, because everything has
> changed. Today the mirror reflects all of
> those characteristics of age that were biding
> their time within that woman of fifty.

My friends don't seem to have had it as easily as I have. They dye their hair odd colours (both men and women) to cover the grey – I discovered, the one time that I tried this, that grey hair is not so easily coloured, and in my case turned to pink. It was an experiment I never bothered repeating. Dyeing hair is to medicalize grey hair as some kind of disease, I feel. My women friends pluck their eyebrows – I pluck my chin hair – and they increase the amount of eyeshadow and mascara they apply in their urgent need to stay young and female until they almost look like transvestites. In my youth, I used face powder, nail polish and eyeshadow until my husband, Eli, in his usual way of asking seemingly naive but often cunning questions, asked me why I was putting plastic on my nails. I dropped all cosmetics cold turkey that day.

The mother of one of my friends spent a load of time putting on her makeup before she would appear in public; even the public of her immediate family. I asked her about this, and she said that she didn't want to cause people the distress of seeing her old and frail. Such a thought would never occur to me. I am what I am and I can't be bothered pleasing other people, protecting them from the knowledge of sickness, old age and death. The effort I save by not bothering with makeup can be used to write a good poem every day and that's what gives me joy. When I am joyful I can help other people be joyful and that is better than defending them from the knowledge that youth will pass.

As one ages, hair does seem to move around the body though. In men it seems to disappear from the top of the head and transports itself to nostrils and ears. In my case the once thick head-hair has moved to the chin. I remember a local Gabriolan doing a monologue on aging and putting in a request that when she was really old would her children please remember to pluck her chin hair. I pluck mine; still having the vestige of the idea that women shouldn't be growing beards.

As far as using perfume to recapture youth, our island is almost a perfume-free zone. The other day someone heavily perfumed sat beside me. At first I was puzzled as to where the smell was coming from so rarely does scent enter the atmosphere on Gabriola; even aftershave and deodorant smells are absent. No, we don't all smell of the sweat of our labours, we have water (however limited in supply it is) and scrubbing brushes.

My husband, Eli, gave me Chanel No. 5 for my birthday. Eli's gifts to me don't usually run to perfume. He is more likely to offer a paper wasp's exquisite little nest, the first flowering branch of our quince tree or a piece of intricate lichen fallen from a log in the woodshed. However, we had recently watched the DVD *Coco Before Chanel,* with the exquisite actress Audrey Tautou. I suppose it was then that I had wished out loud for a bottle of No. 5 for my eightieth. I should mention that this was before I read Hal Vaughan's book *Sleeping with the Enemy: Coco Chanel's Secret War,* which tells of Chanel's Nazi collaboration. I was, of course, surprised at Eli's gift since I knew that nowhere on our small island was Chanel No. 5 available. I had noticed that a small package had been delivered, but ignored it, just telling myself that the Lee Valley catalogue had scored yet once more. As I have to use my perfume discreetly out of the house, I secretly splash it behind my ears when I load the washing machine. It smoothes the laundry process wonderfully.

Does old age have its own smell? I read of the smell of old men and I suppose it is similar to that of anyone who forgets to tend to their teeth, armpits and clothes; but is there a smell of aging and decay such as the one we can smell as plants wither in nature? When I googled for information, I found that there was such a smell produced by the body – it comes from a chemical known as "noneal." The chemical occurs with the breakdown of a fatty acid in the skin, palmitoleic acid. Noneal's smell is a greasy one and chemists call it the natural body odour of aging.

Yes, physical signs of aging do usually creep up on one unawares. Take hearing loss, for example. One minute you miss a few words in a joke that you and your friends are sharing, so you lose the thread of the story, though you laugh uproariously with them to cover; the next, you can no longer hear any of those mournful poets who accompany their words by strumming on a guitar.

It is said that at forty you get your true face, meaning, I suppose, that by that age you have cleared out most of the conditioning your family and life in general has laid on you, and your "true" self has emerged. I know something traumatic happened when I was forty, for it was then that I acquired a new husband, a new career, a white streak in the front of my hair and a pre-cancerous breast lump. But as to gaining my "true" face, I don't know. Martin Amis comments on this rather cynically in his book *Visiting Mrs. Nabokov: And Other Excursions*, "It used to be said that by a certain age a man had the face that he deserved. Nowadays, he has the face he can afford." By the time one is eighty though, I think the real "you" has settled onto your features. The etched wrinkles of frequent smiling or frowning show your tendency to have approached life one way or the other. While your quality of hair may define your state of health, its colour tells of your need to disguise and resist the aging process. The way you hold yourself as you walk tells of your attitude and self-evaluation. Stooped, allows for ideas of life having broken you down. Ramrod, and you have defied the worst. My daughter constantly demands that I put my shoulders back, and gave me the useful bit of advice that this can be achieved by walking forward but pretending you are walking backwards. It sounds paradoxical and impossible, but it actually works.

While we are dwelling on the physicals of growing old, I should remind myself regularly to not dwell on externals. This because I just looked at a photo in one of our local island papers of an older couple celebrating their thirtieth wedding anniversary. They look rather dowdy and definitely corpulent. As I read the article about them I see that thirty-five years ago they won awards for ice dancing. In a flash I have reduced their figures and dressed them in sparkles and yes, yes, I can see them and can join them in celebrating their achievements.

I have a nonagenarian friend who never leaves her apartment unless her hair is just so, her clothes immaculate and her nails...well it's her nails I want to tell you about. I know she has been a gardener in the past, but her hands bear none of the scars that mine have. They have a few pale liver spots on them, but are exquisitely smooth and each finger is tipped with a pale and discreetly pink-varnished nail. Each nail has a perfect moon and the growing edge is perfectly curved. Every time I meet her, my eyes go immediately to her hands. I wonder how many hours a week she spends on manicure and creaming. My hands, however, are not as this. The nails are dirty from garden soil that I can't quite get out, the moons cannot be seen, even on the thumb, since

I never get around to trimming the cuticle, and the general feel of my skin is rough as a dish scraper. I suppose I could write my autobiography using my hands to tell the tales, for one thumbnail is still split down the middle from being shattered when caught in a bread-cutting machine while I was running a youth club in the slums of Birmingham. It was towards the end of my university term and so the thumb was treated both in the university town's hospital and in my hometown hospital, where an ex-boyfriend was lying in a polio cast (this was before polio vaccination) and that introduces altogether different memories from the past. One of my index fingers got spaded by my husband as we frantically dug holes together on a five-acre property we once owned, in order to plant apple trees that had just been torn up when a neighbouring orchard was being bulldozed into the ground. So the thumbnail and the fingernail each bring back a dozen memories when I have to give them attention, which I do frequently since they are split and cause snagging.

From the scar over my eye acquired by bouncing around on my parents' bed when a very young child, to an Achilles tendon scar acquired by dancing the hora too frantically in my middle years, to a lower abdomen scar that I actually cannot remember how it came about, to a recent mastectomy scar, my body is a road map of my life. I chose my hands to trail backwards.

Carolyn Heilbrun, a strong feminist who wrote a mystery series under the pseudonym Amanda Cross, was a blunt woman and she declared her views of the aging woman this way, "I suggested that aging might be gain rather than loss, and that the impersonation of youth was unlikely to provide the second span of womanhood with meaning and purpose."

I myself have little patience with aging people who can't bear looking in the mirror. "Go inside," I want to say to them. "Go inside and dig up something there that is worth looking at. You must have something you value in there. If you can't find anything, change your way of life right now. There's still time to create some worthy image from the bits of your life. I won't believe there isn't. When you've found it, then whatever appears in the mirror you'll realize is merely a fraction of the whole you."

Beach glass

Will someone take me aside now?
> *Now that the tides have*
> *thrown me on beaches*
> *and drawn me under*
> *times beyond count.*
> *Now that the waters*
> *have tumbled me*
> *this way and that,*
> *so the sandstone*
> *has blunted all*
> *sharp edges and*
> *I curl within,*
> *my boundaries softened.*
Will someone take me aside now,
thinking me worth considering
from time to time?

Looking Back

[Memory] is a reconstruction from decaying fragments of the past.... We remember almost nothing of our lives.... Even though memory is tenuous, it is vital. Without it there could be no constructed self at all, only an experiential self, existing only in the present, cut free from all connection to previous or future selves.

– Dr. Guy Brown, *The Living End*

Human beings exemplify a kind of entanglement principle. They say that anyone you have ever entangled with, for good or bad, stays implanted in your memory bank. This principle, I've found, actually has an added corollary, and that is that as these folks from your past pile up inside your brain tissue; they intermingle. It's rather like those Victorian card-books children had in which each page was cut into three, so that you could flip them around and create a figure with a clown's head, a butcher's middle and a knight's armoured legs or many other amusing combinations. This intermingling might be the reason everything seems déjà vu to me these days. With so many images in my memory bank, everything and everybody reminds me of something, or someone else. Why wouldn't they?

A gesture, a certain movement of the limbs, the wiggling of the eyebrows in just that way, sardonic eyelids...all are already registered in our memory storage. So when we meet someone apparently new, we react to them with predetermined behaviour, set according to the first time we met up with such mannerisms in our lives. First impressions of a new person – male/female, body type, racial group, extrovert/introvert, tough/soft, etc. – are based on previous experiences and so action based on those old images may actually be totally inappropriate to the person you are meeting now. They are, however, all one has to work with. One's prejudgments are almost at an animal level; certainly at a tribal one. One is on the alert – prey or predator? Well of course we are civilized and don't like to think we behave like this, but we do.

So all males over sixty-five with shotguns under their arms are classified by one's quick little mind in the same bag of past experiences of men with shotguns, whether the bag contains a shot pheasant, or a shot human; in either case one's hackles are up, at least mine are. You see a young man who looks like a Hollywood star and your mind quickly leaps back to young men of that type you knew in your youth, and so you find yourself greeting him with a certain friendliness, a certain hostility, depending on the memory of the past person that the here-and-now face and pose you are confronting are reminiscent of.

This kind of mental shorthand does serve as a quick rough estimate of how we should react to a new face on the horizon. In Japan one cannot function without business cards, for the card indicates the firm, university, etc., where one is employed, and, more importantly, the position one holds. By looking at the card one can quickly choose the correct level of polite speech with which to address the newcomer. I suppose our mental pictures from the past act in a similar way when helping us access the new face, which in a flash, becomes blended with old faces of a similar nature.

Generic world

When you get to my age,
everything reminds you
of something else…
particularly people,
so that you never react
to newcomers as if they
were fresh experiences;
they remind you of your
first husband, math teacher,
produce manager, father.
It's rather disconcerting
really – as if the whole world
had suddenly become generic.

Memories may, to a large extent, make up our personality. As David Darling said in *Zen Physics: The Science of Death, the Logic of Reincarnation,* "To be a person, one must have a memory – a unique, accessible set of recollections – because to be a person means to hold one's life story and to be actively, intimately involved with it."

Our long-term memory storage seems of infinite capacity and durability. I can remember the licence plate on our old Austin, which I was sitting in when my mother accidentally knocked down a cyclist seventy-six years ago (BHX 954), better than I can recall the video I watched last night. Somehow that stock-bank of memories should be available for us to call upon as we have "the need to re-vision ourselves, to bring all the selves we've known through our lifetime into a new and expanded self, a self that's more than just a collection of losses, one that can live more comfortably in what is inevitably an uncomfortable present." This from Lillian Rubin, in her book, *60 on Up: The Truth about Aging in America.*

But our memories of the past, as Philip Roth reminds us, "are not memories of facts, but memories of your imaginings of the facts." So not only do we select our memories, but we censor and elaborate them as they come into our consciousness. I am reminded here of Beverley George's wonderful tanka:

> family album
> decades of smiling faces
> chart generations –
> not one of us brave enough
> to photograph the tears

As one ages, memory imaginings flood in, in unexpected order and strength. The smallest memory might sweep over one for a whole day, while another powerful one, say from the days of World War II, might just breeze past so that one barely glimpses it.

Nostalgia is what we call memories accompanied by longing. It's as if we are searching for a benchmark, an anchor, a perfect time in our lives that we could somehow reconstruct in the here and now. Wishing to do so can only cause suffering. While remembering happy times and places can give us the courage to go on, getting stuck in nostalgia can only bring about feelings of melancholy, and maybe even depression over the impossibility of ever having those good times again. There's no point in having nostalgia for old times and wishing the present be other than it is. Nostalgia freezes a time which we remember as perfect and suggests it is no longer attainable, whereas memory, while it may also idealize, or at least alter the past, can perhaps show us how firmly our present is indebted to the past. Memory can actually see the past in our present conditions and so is not trapped back then, as nostalgia is.

Anyway, these days most of us have moved so many times, and even changed occupation a few, that recalling a specific time and place worthy of nostalgia is often difficult.

> *this lifetime*
> *of so many moves that when*
> *I have a longing*
> *to go home, I can no longer*
> *recall where it would be*

Oddly enough, when it comes to nostalgia I am often swamped by a general feeling rather than the recollections of specific incidents. And even more strangely, the nostalgia is not always for my own past, but is often for a past completely alien to the events that have actually occurred in my own life. Say, on seeing an episode of *Midsomer Murders* or *Miss Marple*, I have a great urgency to recall someone's life, certainly not my own, in some idyllic English village. A village complete with cottage gardens filled with lavender, thatched roof, Tudor beams and all; the smells of the barnyard; the call of the rooster; the cobbles on the village street; the sweet shop window full of large glass jars of gobstoppers, liquorice allsorts, jelly beans, Black Jacks, Love Hearts, Sherbet Fountain (with its liquorice stick to dip and eat the sherbet) and on the counter there would be boxes of liquorice pipes with red-beaded tobacco burning and liquorice whirls with a candy in the centre. Yes, my nostalgia is all liquorice and lavender.

Other times I can be nostalgic for the twenties in upper New York State as I view sepia photographs of a friend's mother's attic filled with hat boxes and flappers' dresses and chairs where mice have settled in the upholstery. I even wrote a set of poems about this attic, so certain was I that my genes had somehow been there:

> the portrait in the attic
> looks out on the discards
> of other years
> could he have foreseen the neglect
> of things once cherished?

> how oddly sensual
> the curve of a once elegant chair...
> its arms in tatters
> like an older woman, her eyes
> still radiant in her greyness

> perhaps a grandchild's
> fingerprints mark the dusty pitchers,
> their bowls missing, and
> also missing the oak washstand
> on which they once stood ready

sunlight
dusts the chair
so that
the worn arm casts
a worn shadow on the seat

banisters
and fretwork
as new
only the threadbare carpet
tells of the comings and goings

narrow steps
up to the attic and then
a sharp turn
a dangerous corner when
memories call from the upper floor

Paradoxically, with age, while memories can flood in, they can also falter. The most irritating aspect of memory loss as we age is that tip-of-the-tongue temporary failure that allows us to forget names of close friends when we are introducing them, and allows me, when I am signing a new book at a launch on my little island, to completely forget my neighbour's name. This temporary loss has caused me to invent a new kind of game to play at dinner parties. The ones I hold have guests floating around my age and we all suffer from tip-of-the-tongue memory loss. When this occurs I suggest we all rush in with a kind of twenty questions game until, between us, the word is retrieved. I can't tell you how this carries the meal smoothly from course to course.

Recently, someone much younger asked me how it feels to know my past is longer than my future. Not a cruel question, but certainly a penetrating one. I thought a moment and then replied, "Knowing death cannot be far off, each day seems much fuller, much richer, as I seem to now live more consciously than I ever did before. So while it is hard to weigh my eighty years against my next few, my heart tells me the scales may well stay balanced."

Selective Memories

As our long-term memories flood back in detail, we sometimes feel the past is overwhelming whatever future we have left. I like to pretend I still have control over some aspects of my life, and so I have taken to organizing my memories as it were, making some line up on the right, and some on the left, and placing a whole pile in the very centre. In this way they feel non-threatening, and I can even welcome them back from time to time without fear that they will deprive me of my present. The way I am sorting those memories from long ago, whose fine details I recall better than I can what I did yesterday, is by subject matter. Perhaps you are an organizing kind of person yourself, and would like to have a say in what pops back into your consciousness from the past and what doesn't. If you are, I offer here a couple of examples of how I do it. The first is a gathering of my memories by recalling poetry that I have loved over the years, and the second is a flashback by colours. Colours are a sensing matter for me and keep me firmly grounded in the present, while I freely roam in the past.

Let's start with poetry. As a writer, when I have a new book out, it means that my publisher requires that I go on the road for promotional purposes. So, recently, I found myself reading at a local library. A poetry group was meeting and I had been invited to join them. I expected the usual modest crowd elbowing each other as to who would go on first and read their newly minted poems. It didn't turn out that way. After my reading as the invited poet of the evening, the audience members each came forward and read, not from their own writing, but from their favourite poets from the past; poems written by others.

I sat transfixed, listening to poems I had not heard read aloud since my high school days. Wordsworth's "I Wandered Lonely as a Cloud"; Yeats' "The Lake Isle of Innisfree"; Hopkins' "Pied Beauty"; and Davies' "A Great Time." I actually felt tears swell my eyes as the poems triggered memories. I just let go and wallowed in the past.

But I have a very practical survival streak under all this sentiment and an idea suddenly occurred to me. Why not, I thought, why not trace peak moments of my own past by routing to them via favourite poems?

The first image that immediately popped into my head was A. A. Milne's poem "Vespers," for it was framed with E. H. Shepard's wonderful illustration, and hung above my twin's and my own childhood beds. Ours was not a religious household, and I was never taught to pray, yet there was something in the "Droops on the little hands little gold head" that stirred a response within me. Mostly, I think now, it was for the desire to have an ordinary family, with a middle-class home and daily rituals, something I never had. It was years later before I found out that the childhood of

A. A. Milne's son, Christopher Robin Milne, had been even messier than my own.

Tennyson's "The Lady of Shalott" haunted my adolescence, when I loved, from afar, a series of totally unsuitable older boys, just as The Lady had her web shattered by a glimpse of that idiot, Lancelot.

When I immigrated to North America, it was Dorothy Parker's brief witticisms that held my imagination – "men seldom make passes / at girls who wear glasses" kind of poetry. Then, of course, there was Ogden Nash's brilliant wordplay such as rhyming "obstetrician" with "lobstertrician" and "parsley" and "gharsley" and his hatred of metaphor in his wonderful poem "Very Like a Whale," which was possibly a factor in me writing haiku many years later, where overt metaphor is totally absent.

Such poems as Emily Dickinson's "To make a Prairie" reminded me what an immense and varied landscape Canada has; the country I had chosen to adopt as my new home.

I have recently come across a copy of Dr. Seuss' *Green Eggs and Ham*, which saw me through early motherhood, delighting both me and my children, but, when wifedom and motherhood became jail-like, I recited Stevie Smith's "Not Waving but Drowning," which led me to rebirth in Zen koans and the poetry of Rumi.

During my second marriage, life in rural surroundings became a reality as Eli and I built an earth-sheltered house together guided by the nine bean rows in Yeats' "The Lake Isle of Innisfree." When rural life became too burdensome, we travelled, and I, nostalgically, became Padraic Colum's "An Old Woman of the Roads" as I longed for a home, any kind of a home, to put an end to our meanderings. Japan became a temporary home and haiku and, later, tanka became my favourite poetry forms for expressing myself, and Narihira's death poem began to haunt me:

> I have always known
> that at last I would
> take this road, but yesterday
> I did not know that it would be today.
>> (translated by Kenneth Rexroth)

Eventually, on finding and settling in a small house on a reasonable piece of ground, within a fine, supportive island community, Billy Collins' witty poetry and Wisława Szymborska's brilliantly honest poetry helped me find my own poetic voice and integrity, as in:

> *at the bank*
> *the teller discusses*
> *layoffs*
> *I'm secure in the thought*
> *"I live by my poetry"*

Recently I read Alberto Manguel's *Stevenson Under the Palm Trees*, the story of Robert Louis Stevenson's last days. I recalled Stevenson's wonderful Requiem, which is written on his gravestone:

> Under the wide and starry sky,
> Dig the grave and let me lie,
> Glad did I live and gladly die,
> And I laid me down with a will.

This be the verse you grave for me:
Here he lies where he longed to be,
Home is the sailor, home from sea,
And the hunter home from the hill.

This wandering through the years with poetry has probably brought up a lot of odd lines that have stuck in your mind too, tying past events in your life to poetry. I do hope so.

Colours work differently as memory triggers. I named my son Adam, for he who named things in the Bible (including Eve, apparently). I wonder if I did that because I'm so good at naming things myself – my poetry, my essays, my husband's sculpture, others' artworks. Next lifetime I have decided to get a job with a paint company and name their paints – parsley (green), summer haze (blue), keyboard (black), Brideshead (white), damson (purple). Yellow? Why yellow I would like to name "womb." I have a personal reason for choosing "womb" and it may not resonate with the paint-buying public. The reason I would choose womb as the name for a yellow paint is because I wore the most beautiful yellow coat while I was pregnant with my daughter. It formed a cosy womb for me as I offered my womb for her growth. The coat was not the cheerful yellow of kitchens, nor the pastel yellow of baby's rooms where the parents don't want to show the blue and pink distinctions of sex. It was a pale lemon, and the fleecy texture gave it a white glint, that made it even more distinctive. I was so happy in that coat – a wife, and a second-time mother-to-be. All ambitions fulfilled save those of being a writer.

Recently I wrote a book for children on haiku. My very same daughter, now a graphic artist, laid it out and chose a bright yellow for the cover. It was a much deeper colour than that coat that had protected both of us so many years ago, but nevertheless a reminder, as we shared the book's production together.

When it comes to red, I've always managed to have a touch of it somewhere in my life to liven grey days. One red incident happened during a past November, when the pickings of flowers in the garden were sparse. Still, I needed an arrangement for a dinner party, and so ventured out with my secateurs. Nothing caught my eye, and I was about to give up when I suddenly noticed that the dwarf Japanese maple had shed its leaves. A mass of brilliant red covered the ground. I cast the secateurs aside and picked up a handful of the maple leaves. I remember that they were wet from recent rain, but not sodden. They felt delicate and almost affectionate in my hand. I put them in my basket and I quickly cut some parsley, that had gone to seed from a nearby bed.

In the house, I recall placing the red leaves in a shallow celadon dish and sticking sprigs of parsley around the edge. The leaves glowed red against the green dish, as if I had lit a candle within. How the simple arrangement warmed the supper table. Red is such a welcoming colour on a wet November day that we hardly needed the hot apple juice I had prepared to warm our guests.

Here's a green memory from my stay in Japan with Eli so many years ago. Japanese gardens rarely have masses of colour in them despite the thousands of poems written in homage to the Japanese cherry blossom. Green is the essence of a Japanese garden; one's interest is held by the form of the plants rather than their colour, unlike English herbaceous borders.

The word for garden in Japan is *teien*. When written, it is made up of two Chinese symbols, one meaning a ceremonial ground and the other a place where plants are grown and watered. Whether spiritual or not, it is hard not to be immediately transported outside one's daily routine when one views the masses of different greens in a Japanese garden. When you view a moss garden, or a clump of rarely flowering bamboo, or a twisted pine tree, something of awe comes over you that calls on a matching silence within.

When it comes to blue, my memories switch immediately to my adolescence in England. Oxford and Cambridge University rowing colours are dark blue and light blue respectively. Though the product of a red-brick university myself, following the annual rowing race between these two universities was part of my upbringing. Light blue and dark blue were also the colours of my school uniform. It consisted of a strange dark blue, winter, fez-like hat and a matching dark blue coat of nap, a blazer with striped edging of the two blues and a tie that also alternated light and dark blue stripes. In summer, my twin and I wore some wretched pale-blue dresses that my mother had dredged up from somewhere. I suppose that with wartime restrictions spilling over into post-war, I should have been grateful that she managed to get anything together. It was years after I left school before I would wear anything blue again. I had been blued out.

Those memories of my adolescence reminded me of one involved with the colour black. At sixteen, I was gawky, naive, provincial and still wore navy bloomers. We, my twin and I, had been invited to a cousin's twenty-first birthday party in Manchester, a place of culture a few notches up from our honky-tonk town of Blackpool, which was best known for its tourists, its rock candy, its dirty postcards and the Tower Ballroom.

It was shortly after the end of World War II and austerity was still around, but you'd think our mother would have been able to come up with something better than floral cotton, with puffed sleeves and no sign of décolleté. She didn't. On the party night we slipped shyly into the party room where the record player was blaring away and everyone was dancing. All the girls, to the very last one, had on little black dresses, some with the additional sophistication of a string of pearls. We both looked as though we had just walked through a rose garden and the flowers had jumped onto our cheap, shapeless cotton dresses.

Our cousin politely danced with each of us in turn, and then, since no one else seemed to want to, we fled weeping to the guest bedroom, where we sobbed endlessly about our inappropriate clothes and the general awkwardness of it all.

These days, though still naive, I am no longer socially awkward and I have at least three elegant black outfits that Chanel would have given her nod of approval to.

When it comes to white, how stark it seems in one's wardrobe. I'll never forget the turmoil I experienced when I first saw Kazimir Malevich's painting *White on White*. It was hanging at the Albright-Knox Art Gallery in Buffalo, New York. My first husband had introduced me to abstract art, and the simple designs of the Bauhaus school, but white on white was more minimal than I had ever seen. The experience stayed with me when I saw later artists such as Agnes Martin, whose white paintings barely had tracings of her hand on them. The sheer audacity of putting white on a canvas already white! These artists' almost Zen emptying of their canvases must have made me yearn for such simplicity. Only years later, when I lived in Japan, and started writing haiku, did I pare myself down enough to more fully be able to experience the depths of a white painting on a white canvas. I truly realized then, as Rauschenberg said, "a canvas is never empty."

I rarely wear orange and I can't honestly remember when I last saw anyone else in orange either. Burnt orange, with its pleasant autumnal association is occasionally seen, but blazing orange has always been too blatant for my rather shy personality.

In spite of this, a few years ago, I chose to blaze in orange. I had just written a book, *A Gabriola Year*, about my years on my small island. I decided to do the launch at The Gabriola Commons, a piece of property that is held in common by the citizens of Gabriola. The book arrived on time; the illustrations by my daughter, Beverly Deutsch, were witty; the day was sunny; and the large audience was welcoming. Most of them had sat at our kitchen table at one time or another. There's nothing like launching a book on home ground. So, for such a successful combination of factors, I decided to go for orange. The sleek long skirt was a gift from my twin sister and the elegant long tunic topping it, a gift from an old friend, who also donated orange and gold earrings.

Oddly enough, I didn't feel the colour obtrusive, too invasive or too noisy. I felt as though I was truly at home – my home ground, my community, my book, my very own voice at last discovered, my orange outfit... They all fit together perfectly.

Love in our household is not expressed by expensive gifts of jewellery, or cruises in the Caribbean. It finds its way into the extra care with which I iron my husband's shirt cuffs, or my willingness to get into bed first and warm up the sheets on a cold night. Eli, on his part, sends me emails of articles he thinks I might like to read, or he orders books from the library that he thinks will be of interest to me. We rarely use those three little words others find so precious.

Harvest time, rather than the more conventional springtime, is when our love seems to be overflowing as Eli brings the fruit in from the garden for winter storage and I prepare it for the drying trays or the stewing kettle. As team-workers, we best tell of the amount of affection we have for each other.

I recall a day one year when he brought in the first ripe plum; it could be considered a moment of high ardour. I set it, in all its purple glory, on a green plate and we admired it throughout the meal. For dessert, Eli cut it carefully in half and we shared it, the juice running down our chins a little. Purple passion you might call it.

My memories of brown are more current ones. My first husband introduced me to abstract art, my second, to wood. His idea of security is a woodshed stacked with wood for heating the home and a basement stored to the ceiling with wood for his intricate sculptures. Using only close-grained hemlock, still his pieces run the gamut of browns from pale tan to warm caramel, with occasional streaks of cinnamon and coffee.

In the woodshed, the fir, maple and arbutus chunks are stacked in such an interesting order that the whole shed might well be considered an art installation piece, with the boxes of fine kindling twigs acting as staccato accents. Yes, brown is really the colour of the home and of security.

I rarely wear gold. It has always seemed an unpleasant colour to me. This, despite the fact my favourite folk tale as a child was Rumpelstiltskin, where the miller's daughter spun straw into gold. This tale to some extent determined the rest of my life, for I have always been able to spin/knit/sew other people's castoffs into useful objects for our home and have also taught, both myself and others, how to transmute and spin eccentricity into creativity.

Gold reminds me too much of greed and the endless countries raped in order to obtain it. When it comes to gold and greed, think of King Midas and the term "gold digger." Believe me, nothing good ever came from the accumulation of gold.

Silver is my preference for jewellery (although it too is not free of tales of rape and plunder). Walter de la Mare's entrancing poem "Silver" not only captured me with its silvery images when I was a child, but was probably the first poem that made me wonder how poems are made, and intimated to me that I, too, might one day be a poet. Its words were so exciting and accessible. To de la Mare's images of the silver moon glistening on the backs of silver fish, and on the leaves of silver trees, I add, from memories of my years in Japan, that this silvery scene may well have been watched by silver lovers standing on the silver deck of a Heian mansion.

As one of the working titles of this book was "Liquorice and Lavender," I thought I'd recall for you a traumatic incident involving the colour lavender, which, though mild in the ways of world traumas, nevertheless affected me for many years afterwards. It's amazing what big traumas we survive with a certain placidity and which minor ones tip us over into depression.

This lavender memory involved a child who lived down the street from us. I'll call her Yvonne. Her father was a lawyer and she was showered with a host of things that our family couldn't possibly afford. It wasn't her material things that my twin and I were jealous of, however, it was the fact that her parents confirmed that she was okay. They did this, we came to the conclusion in our childlike way, by letting her enter beauty competitions (very prevalent in my childhood) and, most of all, by letting her have dance lessons. My mother, I realized years later, equated dance with sexual looseness and, of course, pregnancy. I recall a dance performance my mother dragged us to in which Yvonne was appearing. There was a number in which all the little girls appeared on stage in one long chorus line. They were wearing crinolines and the crinolines were lavender-coloured. They sang and danced Hoagy Carmichael's "Little Old Lady" and I recall some of the words... You're a perfect picture in your lavender and lace. Well maybe those weren't the exact words, but what we recall may well be more important than the actual event. All that lavender silk material and those little tap shoes and most of all, the applause. Oh, how I longed for it all. Of course, the whole episode is ridiculously trivial, and yet the fact that I wasn't allowed to appear on stage alongside Yvonne, and certainly was not permitted to enter beauty competitions, must have meant that something was wrong with my face and body. This negative image of myself stayed with me into my forties when I finally overthrew it by studying flamenco dancing (red shoes and frilled dress included) six nights a week, and encouraging endless admirers. Memories are tinged with colour and colour is a wonderful hook to bring them into recall.

Palimpsest

My life's a palimpsest.
The calmness of old age,
set clearly in black and white,
punctuated only with
the irritations of "maybes,"
gives way, on scraping,
to a pregnant being,
cells swollen with creation,
and, before that, the potential,
which, on further scuffing,
reveals, in scriptio inferior,
a small child, eyes big
with questions...
"Why something instead of nothing?"
"And before God...?"

And when the parchment,
now so thin and fragile,
would seem close to breaking,
a final first image emerges
of a newborn child,
whimpering continually
for a lost womb companion,
and already pondering
the quest of re-entering Paradise.
And all this faintly pushing

through to the parchment surface...
if one looks closely enough.

Waking as an Older Person

I am lucky that in these, my later years, I do not have to leap out of bed to attend to a baby crying, children to be fed and sent to school, or a husband who might need help with finding clean socks and departing for work (for mine, being a sculptor, has the "wealth of time," as he puts it). Nor do I myself feel the call to labour unless I happen to have a deadline looming, or a reading or workshop for which to prepare.

My husband rises an hour or so before me. He likes to spend the early hours not reading the daily news, but perusing articles on science, or listening to one of TED's many brilliant lectures. Those he thinks might interest me he forwards over to my machine, so that when I check my emails on rising, they are punctuated with interesting things to read, or listen to, apart from the worries of the world. As Eli gets up, I may be awake enough to catch him getting out of bed and glimpse the creaking body that once could do a hundred push-ups without groaning totter towards the bathroom. I smile tenderly and then drift back to complete a dream. A good death, I often think would be, as William Cullen Bryant put it, "Like one who wraps the drapery of his couch / about him, and lies down to pleasant dreams." When the dream closes, I lie for a while wondering where its images came from, my lids still heavy with them. Then, gradually I become aware of the sense of the morning – the curtains shifting gently with an early breeze, the light dancing on the cupboard door as the branches of the cedar tree outside cast a shadow play on them.

I lie awake, aware of the luxury of clean sheets, of a mattress that floats me away each night, of the quilt and the many hours I had put into it, gathering scraps from my own store of worn linens and from those of my friends. I am constantly aware of my luck in having such small luxuries as a change of sheets and the warmth of quilts, and this awareness is accompanied by a feeling of sadness that so many people in the world do not have even these few things. It puts a limit, an edge on my pleasure that is not unwelcome.

As my lids totally unstick, and I give a full-body stretch to make sure everything is still in place, my Puritan instincts unstick also, and I start to plan my day. I do this every morning before I rise as if to make the uncertainty of the day a little less threatening. My husband calls it my secretary mode and dislikes it.

As one ages, change, particularly startling change, is less welcome. Routines offer the illusion that one is still in control of something. Eli and I seem to have more and more routines in order that between the two of us all the necessary chores are covered. I start by planning the two large meals of the day and sort through the fridge while still under the covers. Then I consider household demands – laundry? Time to wash some windows? Work trousers to mend? If the time of year is right there are gardening and food-preserving demands too. But often the words for a poem, or the idea for an essay override all these. Then I go over the lines that have sprung into my mind, again and again, before turning to record them on my bedside writing pad. To wake with a poem entirely formed is the greatest joy for me.

Now, fully awake, I don't delay any further but pause just one moment for my daily *memento mori*. A morning meditation on death tends to speed the urgency of the day. As Carolyn Heilbrun said, "the piercing sense of 'last time' adds intensity, while the possibility of 'again' is never quite effaced." As friends drop away around me; the necessity not to waste a single moment becomes apparent, for who knows whether this will be my last day. The importance of the day does not necessitate a rushing around, a filling of the day with useless stuff, but it does demand a certain intensity – an intensity of my pleasure with the simple food I serve, an intensity of gratitude towards my husband who has put up with my mercurial character all these years, and gratitude too for such things as hot, clean water for bathing, and cold, clean water for drinking, for those are a scarcity for so many. I can join Geoff Dyer when he says that "I have also been able to live on very little money without any sense of sacrifice (a valuable skill, almost a privilege, for anyone wishing to become a writer)." Yes, I too have been likewise privileged. Every day I wake with a thankfulness, for though the past has not always been smooth, I have somehow got to this moment, almost intact in body and the same for my mind, and rich, so rich, rich enough in things that really matter, so that I feel able to share my small largesse with the coming day.

The Quality of the Day

Consider

the quality of the body
floating on solidity and
bent into the familiar mattress;
the quality of crisp-ironed sheets
their reassuring contact and
their smell of ozone.

Consider

the quality of the table
brightened with early crocus
and with a cloth patterned
with late-blooming flowers;
the quality of a sunny side up egg
nestling in garden-lettuce foliage.

Consider

the quality of the desk
polished by papers
inviting words to tumble out;
and the quality of the hesitation,
increasing the pleasure of
the prison-released words
when they finally spill forth.

Consider

> *the quality of twilight*
> *with gauze curtains shifting lightly,*
> *the shadows making the familiar*
> *fresh with unfamiliarity;*
> *the rising moon balancing the ledger*
> *of the quality of the day.*

Generational Warfare

We are stuck inside the dining room of our expensive retirement village. Our suites run out from the dining room like the arms of a prison building, but we cannot get to them. Outside the floor-to-ceiling windows of the dining room are seemingly hundreds of teenagers, while some slightly older people appear to be there too, possibly their parents. They are all carrying banners and raising fists and picking up rocks, but our hysterical cries from inside the dining room must surely out-noise them for we are scared. Our waitresses have turned the tables on their sides as some kind of defence and the pristine white cloths are sagging on the floor like discarded bridal gowns. We have tried to exit the room but the crowd has taken over the lobby and, from the sounds of it, have started to trash our luxury suites. The few men present in the dining room have stalwartly picked up knives and forks as weapons should the windows break and yes! There's the first rock and it has cracked a pane and oh! oh! oh!

Luckily the scenario above hasn't happened yet, and is possibly never going to come about if politicians can think of anything but protecting their own seats. Unfortunately, this condition does imply that it may very well occur as nothing seems to be happening to correct the enormous gaps in wealth and political power between the baby boomers entering the pensionable age and the youth pushing into adulthood. These disparities may well create outraged antagonism on the part of the younger generation as levels of unemployment increase and income supports for them fade.

The gap? This will be the first generation where the offspring will be earning less than their parents. In 2004, the median net worth of a person 55–59 years old was $249,700 and the 35–39-year-olds who were contributing heavily to the elder's social security had a median net worth of $48,940. And there are around eighty-three million baby boomers waiting to be supported in North America alone! The young folk will never accumulate the wealth of their parents. Nor will they, particularly those with large student loans to repay, necessarily be willing to support them. Younger workers start at wages below the going rate while early retirees get bigger pensions than the new young workers are earning. In the States, when FDR brought in social security, there were forty workers to support each person on social security. Now there are about three. Apparently in the US, for every dollar of tax money spent on seniors, only eleven cents goes to children. As Ken Dychtwald says, "The elderly will have to exercise some conscious restraint and have a renewed commitment to fair play. Otherwise the old will inadvertently demolish the young and harm everyone's future in the process."

The young people don't want quite the same things as their elders. If they did, they would be unlikely to get it. The goals of the two groups seem to be incompatible. The elders want to cling to their entitlements. For example, the rich are still claiming social security pensions and full unpaid health care that they could really finance themselves without even noticing, while the younger generation doesn't want to have big taxes cut into their lower salaries in order to meet these demands. Even when it comes to the medical sphere, the generations' needs vary widely; young people want consistent health care, prevention of illness, and rescue from death in the case of accident or acute medical occurrences. The elderly are more concerned with help during the dying process.

If the younger generation wants more money spent on the environment, or on education, the cuts will have to come from medical services and pensions. It will be a social struggle over limited resources. The older generation, although they have paid into pension funds, have just not paid in enough. The whole business sounds like an evolutionary struggle.

Of course, young stags will always butt antlers with older ones for supremacy, and different generations have always disagreed about many things. However, the gap between the aging boomers and the younger generation is more than this expected behaviour, and more than one would anticipate between succeeding generations. Take the gap between my 1930s generation and the boomers. We still think in terms of duty and working hard for a goal, we had a dream and saved for a rainy day, we supported social programs, we loved Bing Crosby. My husband's boomer generation felt being born was enough justification for entitlements, and that life was an adventure, leisure an aim, and education to any level almost a birthright. They spent, spent, spent, now, now, now, while my generation (the one before theirs) saved, saved, saved against another depression; we dug victory gardens and gave our scrap metal to the war effort. The boomers are the Elvis generation. Meanwhile the up and coming X, Y and Z generations move from one job to another with aplomb. They were born with computers in their cribs and communication is their sustenance. They are more assorted than liquorice allsorts packages. The boomers blame my generation for wars; calling us the "Silent Generation." The Xers blame the boomers for increasing divorce figures, global warming, prevalent drug addiction...you name it.

One generation will always blame another, but this time one generation could ruin another as they compete for the same limited resources. The industrial revolution was the time when young people started to move from the farm to the city for work, giving rise to the nuclear family. It has exacerbated the current generation gap, as has the fact that home and work are now separated. The veneration of youth has replaced the veneration of age (if that ever happened) and the emphasis on individual achievement has replaced any community feeling with high competitiveness (and as jobs become scarce that means competitiveness between generations).

To prepare for old age in a settled family-oriented rural community is much easier than for isolated elders living in wretched rooms in a city's core. In such situations the ownership of wealth is the only assurance, and a very weak one too, that one will be cared for and respected in one's old age. In the detective story *The Black Cat* by Martha Grimes, the detective thinks, "People fell into condescension so often with the old, but not always with the old and rich."

Such wisdom as the elderly once handed down to the younger generation in an agricultural community is no longer needed in a fast-changing technological and information age. Not only do the generations not mix as much as they used to because of the nuclear family that city life has produced, but the information that was once handed down the generations is now of little relevance. Even the fact that there are now far more aged people around means that they are not as revered as when, say, to be eighty was a prodigious thing. Younger people are much harsher in their judgements of the aged than they were. For example, if an old person is decrepit now, rather than being pitied, they are blamed for their profligate habits or unhealthy lifestyle that has brought on such illnesses.

Younger people begin to see older people as different from themselves and almost cease to identify them as humans, clumping them together in some kind of homogeneous grouping. But old people are not homogeneous; they are not only different from young people, but they are also different from each other. They are individuals, but then so are young people. If only the two generations could be brought to look at each other with more understanding of their different needs, that understanding could surely work for the benefit of the whole population.

Will there be a generational war? Already the young are getting edgy about the inadequate (and possibly non-existent) pension funds for their future, and that, in the near future, two of them will need to somehow finance one retiree. Susan Jacoby says, "Anyone who expects young adults, most of whom cannot even imagine illness, much less death, to forgo today's pleasure so that they can pay for their own long-term care [or anyone else's long-term care, come to that] in their nineties does not have a realistic view of human, or at least American, nature."

Many media people forecast bankruptcy, or at least stagnation of the economy brought on by the greying, balding population. Theodore Roszak counters all this criticism by calling the aging generation "the best educated, most socially conscientious, most politically savvy older generation the world has ever seen." Other writers also hold out some hope. They suggest what I call Vajrayana solutions. That is, somehow converting the problem into the solution. In this case, the problem of health care costs, if viewed from a different angle could result in the industrial revolution being replaced by the health care revolution...the economy becoming based on health care providers.

When it comes to face-to-face relationships between the different generations, the fracture remains though – the children are in daycare, the elderly in isolated condos, or retirement or nursing homes. Friendship and understanding cannot come about by one hour a week planned mixing.

My mother in her mind-wandering last years redid the family albums. She cut out her son-in-law (the one who had committed adultery) from all the photographs that he had occurred in and mixed all the seaside-sand-and-small-children shots together so that I and my twin as infants on the beach at Yarmouth are mixed in with shots of my own children when we were seasiding at Cape Cod and Mount Desert Island each year. I wonder whether the generations couldn't in some way also be mixed and sit happily side-by-side as they did in my mother's photo albums?

Generation Gap

Tight within a tradition,
bounded firmly with belief
and blinkered with custom,
all curtains drawn on options,
one generation blends into another
seamlessly, without a sliver of change.

But when the blinds are up,
things move so rapidly that
one moment hardly resembles
the next, and a day can turn
the world upside down.
In such a confusion, what
have grandparents to say to grandchild?
Even their own children speak
a foreign language and live
in alien rooms where grandparents
cannot tell what is in the cupboards.

What to Call Us?

We are not "senior citizens" or "golden-agers." We are the elders, the experienced ones; we are maturing, growing adults responsible for the survival of our society. We are not wrinkled babies, succumbing to trivial, purposeless waste of our years and our time. We are a new breed of old people.

– Maggie Kuhn quoted in *Maggie Kuhn on Aging,*
edited by Dieter Hessel

Well maybe. I think the odds are that the majority of folks in the world over seventy lean towards the things Ms. Kuhn says we are not. Perhaps she was just speaking about herself and not owning it. Authors often do that; that is, put their own opinions into the general public's mouths. I myself, at eighty, am wrinkled, and while I don't waste all of my time, I often tend to watch two DVDs a night, and sometimes they turn out to be worthless. Who *is* Ms. Kuhn talking about, I wonder? I read that the average retiree watches forty-three hours of television a week, and is in what Dr. Dychtwald calls "an elder wasteland."

Many of my friends have not matured noticeably in the years I have known them; I really have not done much in the way of maturing myself. Forgive the aside but I just came across a nice definition of maturity, or at least of "growing up" – "Knowledge is not all relative. Some knowledge is more reliable than others. To accept that fact is called growing up." This quote is by Chet Raymo. Many of my contemporaries have become emotionally and physically dependent on a partner and take no interest whatsoever in outside events. They are ordinary, everyday older people, and I think Ms. Kuhn is just another idealist backing human nature, when there is little evidence that it is evolving anywhere near as fast as the technology that makes our aging a little less painful.

Advertisements in magazines for over-fifties these days are for the most part about leisure cruises, a variety of pensions, how to handle your investment portfolio, luxury retirement communities, luxury nursing homes and the display of expensive gewgaws. The magazines do not seem to cover interesting and stimulating books, or have articles about inhumanities that can be spoken out against or human rights that need defending. I should be generous and hope, with Ms. Kuhn, that mature elders are coming just around the corner, but I'm not hanging around to see them arrive. As sharp-tongued Susan Jacoby points out, "Since both profound wisdom and common sense are in short supply at any age, it seems illogical that these desirable qualities should manifest themselves more frequently among those of advanced age."

On the other hand, I also know centenarians who can discuss the situation in the Middle East in depth, and folks in their eighties who are potting and painting and sculpting as professionals and protesting a load of injustices. But I prefer to present the whole picture, and not dwell too long on a kind of homogenous, wise elder society emerging. They may, as a group, have increasing money and the power that goes with it, but it's unlikely they'll have the wisdom to share this willingly with other age groups. It ain't going to happen without some kind of struggle.

I wonder whether gurus such as Ms. Kuhn don't tend to gloss over details, for next I read Zalman Schachter-Shalomi and Ronald S. Miller in *From Age-ing to Sage-ing: A Profound New Vision of Growing Older* denying what is totally apparent to anyone going where the snowbirds go in the winter. "Elder citizens," they say, "are *not* 'senior citizens' who get gold watches at retirement, move to Sunbelt states, and play cards, shuffleboard, and bingo *ad nauseam*." Well that's exactly what a bunch of them are doing, and what's wrong with that? We all have to go, and we can all choose the path we want to take – to a certain extent.

By the way, it was Joy Elmer Morgan who introduced the words "senior citizen." Of it she says, "The term 'senior citizen' is intended to describe a mature, responsible, spiritually self-disciplined person who has control of his present and future existence.... Failure to face the later years and to plan for them is a sign of infantilism and immaturity." There you go! Another idealist who can't see the state of most of the over-sixty-fives around her.

Still the age group seventy to a hundred is a new group that barely existed one hundred years ago, so what to call us? Peter Laslett, the authority on the "third age," defined the four ages of life as follows: childhood, working and family, freedom from work and family, decrepitude and death. Well, it hardly needed a doctorate to divide life up like this. By the way, adolescence, which seems to be included in childhood by Mr. Laslett, didn't exist as a category before the twentieth century. When students started to go to high school, the group there developed their own behaviour codes and this resulted in a recognition of the hormones-running-wild stage, which had previously been channelled into early marriage and parenthood. I do rather like Goldie Hawn's division for women (à la Hollywood) – "Babe, District Attorney and Driving Miss Daisy." This does make me wonder as longevity increases, what will be the new life-stage markers?

The third age, which I seem to be living in now since I am still writing for a living, although decrepitude is rapidly intruding, is nicely defined as "freedom from…" However, being self-employed, I continue to pressure myself with the same puritanical intensity as when I desperately needed an income, so really there is not much difference between my third age and my second age with the exception that my adult children are supporting themselves.

"Third age," I think, is not generally an adopted designation, but what to call us "freedom from work and family" folks in non-Laslett terms? Mature is nonsense, as I have met some toddlers more mature than some of my contemporaries when it comes to cleaning up after themselves and taking responsibility for their actions. "Elderly" implies a certain lack of vigour, which is true on some days for me, but not on all days. "Senior citizen" is vaguely patronizing, as if making up for the fact we don't count for much in junior citizens' eyes – overcompensating as it were.

On our island, Gabriola, amongst the New Age bunch, "elders" is definitely in. It implies a certain respect, even reverence, and the image of me sitting in a position of power among a circle of "youngers" has a certain appeal. However, on the whole, I find "not so powerful" is usually the more comfortable position for me to be situated in these days, so "elder" does not sit totally well with me. My island also has a penchant for the word "crones" and even had a showing of crones' art. I participated in this, not because I consider myself a crone, but because I wanted to appear with a bust Nancy Crozier had made of me from shredded copies of my books which she had bought. It was a severe form of criticism, I thought, but loved that you could read my publisher's name over my eyebrow, and lines from my poems creased my face. Crone is defined as "an ugly, withered old woman; a hag" and I can't believe our New Age islanders meant that usage. More likely they were using it to name post-menopausal women who are both empowered and wise. Alright, I'll go along with that.

Definitely out for some are "old" and "older," which ring of senility and things geriatric, and the designation "fifty-five, or better" is just plain stupid. "Centenarians" seems straight talk for those of you who are one hundred and, if one is over that mark, then "super-centenarians" appears to be the latest label. Nicole Hollander, who writes wittily about old age, says she would ban *"old bitty, crone, dried-up prune, senior moment, oldster, geezer, old geezer, old duffer, old-timer, duffer, golden-ager, dotard, doddering,* even *veteran"* from being used. She does favour *doyenne,* however, which would actually well describe her. By the way, thanks to Ms. Hollander drawing my attention to the words, I have just learned that "gaffer" and "fogey" were once terms of respect. Other discriminatory words used, this time specifically for older boomers, are "aging boomers," "grey tsunami," "ticking time-bombs," "greedy geezers," and "economic burdens." Betty Friedan coined the more positive words "biological pioneers" for baby boomers since their very much extended old age scarcely existed before.

In *Age Beat: The Newsletter of the Journalists Exchange on Aging*, journalists are advised "Use [elderly] only as a modifier (e.g., *elderly people, elderly patients*) in referring to *people who are discernibly old and frail*" (italics added). And in a recent report overseen by Robert Butler of the International Longevity Center the recommendation is that, "If you need to identify individuals over the age of 50, 'older adults' is preferred over 'senior' and 'elderly,' which can be discriminatory in nature... Instead, say 'man' and 'woman,' and give the age, if relevant to the story." As I write occasionally for a magazine called *Senior Living* that has a large readership, none of whom apparently object to the magazine's title, this leaves me in a certain perplexed quandary when it comes to writing about people around my age. And while we are speaking of how older people are reported in the press, Lillian Zimmerman in her excellent book on moving on from middle age, *Bag Lady or Powerhouse?: A Roadmap for Midlife (Boomer) Women*, wonders why an incident reported in a paper mentions X as a grandmother, when X's actions have nothing to do with grandparenting.

Lillian Rubin in her book, *60 on Up* cites a Harris Poll as saying that "most people over sixty-five resist euphemisms such as 'senior citizen' or 'mature Americans' almost as much as they do terms like 'old,' 'older Americans,' and even 'retired Americans.'" Ms. Rubin concludes that "there is currently no language in this society that will reduce the stigma of age and, therefore, none that the old will wear comfortably." Jack Rosenthal agrees, and suggests, "There is probably no single acceptable term – because no single term can embrace so vast and varied a population. The ultimate answer will most likely be a suite of functional and factual terms, like the typology scholars use to distinguish between the *young-old*, 65 to 80; the *old-old*, 80 to 90; the *oldest-old*, 90 to 99; and *centenarians*. Terms like these, though somewhat awkward, are apt to enter common usage as society faces up to the new age of age. Necessity is the mother of locution."

I discussed this naming problem with my husband, Eli, who had just received his Gold Card. "Why do we have to be called anything?" was his reply. As usual his ability to see through labels puts a fresh perspective on everything. As human beings first, talents, sex and age considerations later is how people should be defined, if they have to be defined at all, I feel.

Perhaps a sign of respect such as the Japanese suffix "*sama*" would be a gentle recognition of our age and the esteem we would like to have given to us, recognizing the productive years we may have offered. "Wakan sama" sounds rather splendid, I feel.

A friend just told me of a well-known actor who, when on stage, looks much younger than her actual years. One day she was shopping at a Chinese grocery store, when the grocery clerk bent towards her, examining her face closely and pronounced, "You old!" For the next few weeks she went around saying, "I old." So yes, "I old" makes clear one acknowledges one's years, at least the last half of the phrase does. The "I" is more difficult to define, for although I have a body of skin, flesh and bones as the Buddhists might declare, I am also just a bundle of memories squashed into this instant; a quivering of senses, a linking of neurons. Even science these days is considering the "I" as multiple layers – the inner-monologue self, the view-I-have-of-myself-as-a-person-in-relationship-to-others self, and my external-behaving self, along with other layers, all apparently overlapping and constantly changing. In comparison with defining what "I" might be, giving a name to people of lengthened years should be easy, I would have thought.

I'm a moment

I'm a moment.
A pile of dust
with a point of view.
My ideas? They come
from a command post
far from consciousness.
My feelings, chameleon-like
change as the breezes,
a thousand times a day,
at the slightest nudge,
offence, favour.
There is no substance
to such a being.
I'm just a shifting
with opinions…
a trembling
of trivialities…
yet somehow essential.

In Defence

If your hair is grey, or white as mine is, have you ever had people speak very slowly and loudly to you? Or, worse yet, speak to you as though you had regressed to age six, as an anaesthetist did once to me? If so, they are behaving with the blinkers of stereotyping.

In my reading in preparation for this book I came across a remarkable number of stereotypes of older adults. I know they are generalities, nevertheless they are often quoted generalities and, as I read them, I felt I should rush to my own, and my peers' defence. I will start by listing the ten most common opinions younger folk have about us, mostly given by the eighteen to thirty-five bunch. We are:

1) Fuddy-duddies – conservative, resistant to change and new technologies, behind the times, inflexible, too dependent on routines, cowardly, unwilling to take risks.

2) Penny-pinching, mean, miserly.

3) Not up to the job (whatever "the job" might be) and losing it (whatever "it" might be).

4) Boring.

5) Cynical and pessimistic.

6) Responsible for bankrupting the economy.

7) Unproductive, worthless.

8) Grumbly, querulous and cantankerous.

9) Selfish – thinking only of ourselves and the moment.

10) Poor listeners and unstoppable speakers.

Well that will do for a start. However, before I begin my defence for our case, and ever conscious that there are always two sides (if not more) to every question, I did pause to wonder about M. F. K. Fisher's rather strong comment that "I have formed a strong theory that there is no such thing as 'turning into' a Nasty Old Man or an Old Witch. I believe that such people, and of course they are legion, were born nasty and witch-like, and that by the time they were about five years old they had hidden their rotten bitchiness and lived fairly decent lives until they no longer had to conform to rules of social behaviour, and could revert to their original horrid natures."

It seems to me that many of the complaints that I've listed are because folks of other ages expect over-sixty-fivers to behave in just the same way as they do. This is not the way it works. As R. L. Stevenson said in his wonderful essay, "Crabbed Age and Youth," it would be "as if a ship captain should sail to India from the Port of London; and having brought a chart of the Thames on deck at his first setting out, should obstinately use no other for the whole voyage." We over-sixty-fivers have our own ways of doing things and they shouldn't necessarily be viewed either negatively, or as pathological behaviour. At our age, why should we be expected to have the same outlook, philosophy, needs and desires of someone in their forties?

Well what can I say in our defence? I can't deny that our hearing and vision deteriorate, our memories falter and our bodies start to slow down. But let's look at these criticisms I've listed above one by one and see how they can at least be met, if not indeed countered.

1) Fuddy-duddy? I've learned that jumping on the latest bandwagon, the latest trend, whether it be length of skirt or being up-to-date about the "in" people of the moment is a waste of energy. The new becomes the old in five minutes these days. Perhaps it's wisdom that allows me to sit out Facebook and Twitter and other recent ways to communicate. I've learned that five good friends are better than one hundred trivial contacts and, since I know the faces of these five so well, why Facebook? Many of us at this later age seek solitude (not to be confused with isolation) and are not constantly diverted by the novel, for, after all, we have seen almost all of it anyway.

As to living in the present, we oldsters have a quality that youngsters might well envy, for we can live in our childhood, our middle age and our old age all at once. They may view us as being confused, but we find that being able to live present and past seemingly all at one time, opens new perspectives on matters that count.

Of course we're more cautious, although I would hardly use the word "cowardly." We're cautious and don't take risks because we have learned, often by bitter experience, of all the things there are to be cautious about out in the wide world.

As Judge Richard A. Posner says, "The old dog is rational in not wanting to take the time to learn new tricks, as the cost will be greater and the benefit smaller than in the case of a young dog.... The older a person is, the more deeply entrenched and hence more costly to change are his practices, attitudes, and responses." This is a straight economics statement by a clear thinker giving one reason why we don't want to 'keep up.'

2) Penny-pinching? How about the fact that either we have everything (not my case) or that we have everything we need (that's more like it), so we don't need to splash money around? I can go a whole week without seeing a shop and, when I do, I have a list of basics I need, so why gather more. More only needs dusting. We have learned how hard it is to earn money, so of course we are careful where and when we distribute it to others. I myself, shopping so seldom, don't bargain-hunt or coupon-shop, but for those who do, they probably have plenty of time and so it may be cost-effective, and even a form of enjoyment for them to spend that time being economical.

3) Not up to the job? We may appear to be doing whatever needs doing more slowly, but perhaps, with our life experiences behind us, we don't need to be so speedy; we've just learned smarter ways of doing things and so can afford to relax and take a bit more time, being assured that eventually we will complete the task well and probably more thoroughly. Losing it? Well, why am I losing it if I can't find my glasses when they are on my nose, when a teenager, if they can't find their hockey puck, is not "losing it"? They probably haven't sorted their room out since last winter. Isn't that "losing it"?

4) If someone isn't speaking of things that interest you, then they may well be classified as "boring" it's true, but this applies to a person of any age.

5) Cynical and pessimistic. Of course we're cynical and pessimistic. What evidence can you produce to give us more faith in humankind? We've seen it all and mostly we don't like it. But we do like the smaller horizons of the world which we have created around ourselves, they are quite enough to keep us going. It is natural that we dwell on present disasters and think that things were better in our youth. Young people naturally are optimistic about their long future ahead, because it is unknown. It is quoted that one in five non-institutionalized older people are depressed. Goodness knows what the ratio for institutionalized folk is then. Judge Posner, in his candid way, suggests that the depressions of old age are not clinical but realistic when considering our "declining quality and prospects of life." Why wouldn't we be pessimistic?

Moreover, as Joan Chittister points out, "No wonder there is a natural melancholy that sets in as the years pass by. The world around us begins to change, and, little by little, the world that shaped us fades away, without so much as a notice, with hardly a nod." So yes, both the state of the outer world plus our definite near future of rapidly declining powers is bound to temper any optimism we might have. As an aside it is said that writing skills decline less with age than other cognitive skills. I am delighted to hear this and note it down immediately.

6) Bankrupting the economy. We are not bankrupting the economy. The banks and multinationals and people who don't pay their income taxes and folks who send their savings offshore are bankrupting the economy. We are swelling the coffers of the retirement villages and nursing homes and medical personnel and pharmaceutical companies and personal trainers and hosts of other people who cater to our needs. Instead of looking on us as vampires, sucking the blood of the health system, why not turn the idea upside down and see how productively we older folk stir up the economy; though admittedly our cash is enriching a specific area – health. It is only a partial defence, but I should mention that Susan Jacoby points out that it was the earlier generation (the Depression generation) that made a lot of money by providing free luncheons to the boomers, that is causing a number of our present economic woes. As she states, "No generation has a monopoly on greed

and stupidity." She adds "financial stupidity" to this judgement.

7) We are not unproductive and worthless. You just aren't taking enough trouble to see what we are producing – the hours of child care we are volunteering (for our grandchildren) and the hours of volunteering in the community, on committees and on fundraising for community needs (worth five billion dollars a year in Canada, apparently – hardly small change). Just because we aren't paid for our services, doesn't mean that we aren't productive. Describing old adults as "worthless" reminds me of Dylan Thomas who wrote about his elderly aunts who were "not wanted in the kitchen, nor anywhere else for that matter." But then Thomas was an extreme scrounger, and lacked any noticeable moral principles as far as I can tell, so who can expect more from him.

8) Ted C. Fishman points out that, "The voices for the elderly are so steeped in complaint that they often seem to be striving to reinforce a stereotype they deplore, that of the elderly as incoherent, ornery, and demanding."

We are not grumbly and cantankerous. We are critical and selective. We want things well done, and well done for us. We no longer need to say nice things when we don't feel them, to smile continually when we don't feel happy, to go places from obligation, to flatter and praise when it is undeserved – all this takes far too much of our precious energy. We can actually be honest all the while now and know the price of others' disapproval at our outspokenness and ornery behaviour is well worth it. Our old masks of social compliance no longer need to be worn and we don't have to keep up a veneer to satisfy the world.

A couple of examples come immediately to mind. Living on a small island, as I do, the first rule on settling in is to keep your mouth closed. I, with much effort at restraint, kept to this rule for many years. Recently, as my inhibitions drop away, I have been behaving more like the child who pointed out that the emperor has no clothes. An example is that a while back, a house burned down on the island because the tenant left her meditation candles burning and went out. I happen to know a small amount about meditation and know its key word is "awareness." The tenant then sent, via the island email SOS, a plea for a new house to rent. I was in a small group when this piece of information was shared and I immediately blurted out, "Who would rent to such a careless person?" This was not the party line on the island where compassion is endless (and uncritical) and there was a somewhat extended silence.

On another occasion, I was again hostess, but this time it was not I who asked the wrong question. Two of the folk visiting didn't know each other and so I introduced them, and, as is the way with introductions, they both summarized their lives in a few sentences. One of my friends in her late seventies then uninhibitedly asked, "Oh, so you married for money then?" This, again was a reasonable question a six-year-old might ask, but not entirely appropriate in a gathering where the answer might spread like fire around the island in less than a day.

One of my favourite books when I was young was Beverley Nichols' cynical book about adults, *For Adults Only*. In it, a child asks the kind of questions I and my friend asked above; logical questions, reasonable questions that any bright child would want answered... only we happen to be seventy years older than that child.

By the way, why can't the elderly be allowed anger? Does it go against our idea of wisdom? Do "satisfactory" older people sit around calmly, expressing balanced and learned bits of advice? Where on earth did that idea come from? Anger is energy and energy repressed causes depression. It's bad enough that we folks in our seventies and eighties have enough real reasons for depression – sadness and regrets, our marginalization and isolation, etc., etc. Depression in the older adult isn't a disease; it occurs because society doesn't provide enough places where we can be fruitful. Why add to that by not allowing us some 'suitable' rage? We are accused of being irritable, when we are not allowed full expression in occasional righteous anger. And there is a lot to be angry about in this world of ours. Our depression is from social suffering. Old folks are expected to withdraw and, I suppose, the ultimate withdrawal is dying. The more we withdraw from society, the less the younger folk have to suffer signs of our decay. If we told openly of this pain, our anger would be released. Anger challenges ageism.

9) We are not selfish and thinking only of the moment,
    any more than the young do. If we think more of the
    present it is because we are "here and now." We know
    to be in the moment is to be in the essence of things.
    If the moment just happens to be revolving around
    us, then that is where our attention demands to be.
    What looks like selfishness is really enlightenment.
    And, moreover, as we pull our horizons in, as our
    energy diminishes, it is natural we should focus on
    matters closer to home. I have some moments, in
    fact, when I have the weird feeling that my past has
    somehow disappeared altogether, and it seems as if
    there is only the "now." It is as if all that has gone to
    make "me" is no longer of importance, the moment
    of the pencil on the paper is all there is. Yet, at other
    times I am so sure that it is my memories that make
    up a good part of who I am.

    Somehow life is paradoxical in that when we are
    in the here and now, the past disappears, but at the
    same time, the deeper we are in the here and now, the
    more we feel linked to ourselves at other ages and,
    indeed, to feeling we are part of a long life process of
    generations. You explain it to me, please.

10) Poor listeners and garrulous speakers. Well there is
    little fresh to be heard and most of it is gossip and
    rumour, so really we don't lose much by not listening.
    I have not obtained a hearing aid on purpose because
    mostly I don't want much input, unless it is editorial,
    and that comes via the machine. As a friend said, "I
    can't imagine anything anyone can say to me that's

worth five thousand dollars" (the cost of hearing aids, which often don't work anyway).

We talk a lot because we have a lot to tell and most of it is fascinating, at least to us. We listen little because we have little time left to rush around adapting to novel situations and exploring the latest whatever we are being told about, so why bother listening to it?

And that, my Lord, is my defence. I rest my case.

The Baby Boomers Grow Up

As I mentioned earlier, my husband is a baby boomer, or rather he was born just one year before the baby boomers burst onto the North American demographical scene in the post–World War II period from 1946 onwards. I myself was a "Depression baby" or whatever incoming infants were called who were born around the 1930s. I was a cheerful Depression child and was rarely conscious, in my enchanted childhood, that our family was hard-pressed financially, as my twin and I trampled in the blackberry patches and roamed the beaches.

Even after thirty-five years of marriage, my husband, fourteen years younger, is a great mystery to me. Sometimes I look at him curiously, wondering whether he came from outer space on some alien spaceship. So, in the interest of keeping those sparks going in our marriage, and in order to see if I could gain some insight into his everyday behaviour, I decided to read some books on the boomers. The books I chose were Ken Dychtwald's *Age of Power: How the 21st Century will be Ruled by the New Old*, Theodore Roszak's *The*

Making of an Elder Culture: Reflections on the Future of America's Most Audacious Generation, and David Willetts' *The Pinch: How the Baby Boomers Took Their Children's Future – And Why They Should Give it Back.*

I believe, as Judge Posner gives evidence for, that "there has never been a society in which old people as a whole have been as politically influential, as materially well-off, and probably as happy, as they are in modern North American society." They own seventy-seven per cent of all financial assets, are sixty-six per cent of all stockholders, own almost half the credit cards in the US, and over seventy-nine per cent of the group own their own homes...the list is endless. Of course this financial statement doesn't assure their happiness, although it does provide hints that their basic needs are being met. I do realize, however, that marginalized older people, such as female immigrants, do not sit in this group of well-provided-for boomers.

Often when you go searching for something, you find something else you weren't expecting. I went to these books searching for clues as to what makes my husband tick and instead discovered that his generation is becoming not only a powerful political force (grey power, as it were), but a force that expects entitlements, and will make sure that they get them. Baby boomers are the first generation that assumed it didn't have to go to work immediately after high school or university, that it was reasonable to change careers as often as they liked, that allowed themselves not to marry the first person who came along, and to delay parenthood as long as they could, so why wouldn't they carry the idea of entitlement into their old age?

Baby boomers have distorted society as they have grown older as a pig would a snake's body that has swallowed it; first with swelling the need for daycare, then classrooms, university places, jobs, and now pushing the health care system and the need for retirement and nursing homes way out of kilter. On top of this, they are demanding that their pensions be maintained, a demand that possibly the upcoming generations may not be able to meet. The baby boomers are going to outlive their pensions and there lies the real problem.

I took a moment to consider the fate of the elderly before pension plans even existed, a thing that I had never looked at before. Those who hadn't piled up worldly goods, or who weren't supported by their children, found their way to the workhouse, or dingy boarding houses where they were barely maintained. We speak of abuse of the elderly now, but it is nothing like the fate that awaited those who couldn't provide for themselves in the early twentieth century. Social security, health care plans and pension funds have changed the economic fate of older people. But have the baby boomers threatened this security safety net then with their bumper stickers announcing that "we are off spending our children's inheritance"?

The baby boomers will be living longer than any previous generation, and they will spend more time being old than they did being young. They could become a centre for economic and political power. Because of this, it is argued that the boomers should therefore change their mindset about how they are going to spend the extra years of their life; and that this is the most important challenge they will ever have to face. The question seems to be whether this generation will use their later years to influence their own entitlements, or whether it is possible that they will have a change of heart and be able to steer their energies into a more compassionate channel?

This, of course, depends on the narcissistic "me" generation of baby boomers moving away from SUVs and other conspicuous displays of consumer goods, and having what one might almost call a spiritual turning so that they can see that their particular entitlements could become "entitlements for all," so that *everyone* becomes ensured of a fair basic wage and possibly a reasonable basic income guarantee. Some think that entitlement for all is possible if the money available for the industrial-military complex could be diverted to peaceful endeavours.

Perhaps this will be possible if the power of the aging baby boomers means the beginning of a gerontocracy willing to take on tasks that are "worth living for and fighting for." Social security, guaranteed Medicare in the United States and health care in general in Canada are the linchpins of this vision. This is a big vision for a society in which the baby boomers have spent thirty, or more, years acquiring things, and whose children are now fated to be earning less than they did. Government and personal financial support in the past used to move from the older to the younger generation; now the flow seems to be in reverse.

A word aside here as I give more thought to this underlying greed of the baby boomers. I realize that this greed is present in all of us. It is called desire – the desire to have pleasant things happen to us and the desire to avoid the difficult and distasteful things that life is apt to throw our way. Desire is a paradoxical thing. It is the desire to live that propels us forward to explore new territories and to conquer new heights. At the same time it is this very same desire that can distort over into endless acquisitions, competitiveness and the major divisions that we are seeing that may very well bring our civilization, as we know it, to an end. As the world's resources appear to be limited and needing of careful allocation, the divisions between the rich and the poor, and the young and the old are becoming harmful divisions that will have to be confronted.

People's life expectancy is growing, there is no doubt about that, and older people will have more and more say in public policy. Even in India, where sixty per cent of the people are presently under thirty, within forty years there will be a gerontocracy. It is being suggested that such societies become health care societies instead of industrial societies. So what if forty per cent of the national income goes to health? If we all live forty per cent longer in a comparatively sane and healthy way, then surely that is a wonderful thing.

The health care industry supports doctors, hospital staff, pharmacies and pharmaceutical businesses, the makers of prostheses, the researchers researching disease, longevity and genetic medicine, insurance companies and all the spinoffs from these. Someone once described this move from industrial and military concerns to health concerns as "turning silver into gold." Isn't that better than supporting armaments or SUVs or the making of unnecessary gewgaws in China? The future's most influential industry could be health – the raw material is ailing and aging and the product is better health and longer lives. As a final spur towards his ideal of a gerontocracy run by the baby boomers, Mr. Roszak agrees with another writer's opinion that "retirement energy is probably the only increasing natural resource."

Reading these books did give me a firm hope that the self-indulgent boomer generation could possibly be transmuted by self-knowledge to use their excellent educations to extend their entitlements to everyone – a call to wisdom and nobility, no less.

My readings also gave me pause to consider the entitlements that baby boomers take for granted, for at the end, I am left with a lingering doubt – doubt as to whether I think everyone should be entitled to a secure old age. How about those who have spent a lifetime of pimping, of drug dealing, or gambling, or in armament dealing, or money laundering, or in extortion; should those kind of folk really be given an old age of entitlement? Is it possible I am a Puritan at heart? Well, possibly. Certainly I seem to be making moral judgements and shamelessly too. Is it really enough that we have been born on this earth to merit us bed and board too? Oh dear! I'm asking impossible questions again. Don't the small words "responsibilities" and "duties" suggest there should be a balance to all these entitlements?

I do wonder why books on the boomers speak so little of responsibilities – responsibility to contribute to one's family, one's community, even one's nation, never mind taking responsibility for one's own shortcomings, not to mention deadly sins.

Altogether another connection I have made through my reading is that since women outlive men, there is the distinct possibility that one day the world could find itself run a little more from a female aspect. That this might be a good thing is only a tentative idea on my part, for Margaret

Thatcher was hardly a good example of veering the world towards compassion. I do also worry that wealthy seniors will abuse their growing power, by not making sure that their entitlements are shared by the whole community, or by using clever tax lawyers to avoid paying what they can afford to pay, such as avoiding nursing home costs by changing title to property and other juggling of assets. Oh dear! Why don't I stop worrying about such petty matters and give the vision a chance?

Baby boomers may own a good chunk of our country's wealth, but they also consume seventy-four per cent of prescription drugs and use up sixty-five per cent of all hospital bed days and over three million of them (in North America) are either in nursing homes or continuing care and assisted living residences. That is, they contribute, but they also make demands which can only increase drastically in the next decade. These demands include those on health care; demands for anti-aging techniques; demands that technological improvements speed up so that they can assist the aged more and sooner; adjustments to insurance and retirement plans; the need for appropriate housing and transport; provision of leisure time activities; training for possible re-employment (a comparatively new phenomenon); and, of course, that more support be offered during the period of dying. Dychtwald points out that almost nothing has been done to meet any of these looming needs and I'll take a look at this situation in the next chapter.

"And Eli?" you will ask. "Have you gained any new insights into your baby boomer husband?" Well one thing did become clearer in all that reading, and that is that baby boomers *workshop* everything. That is, Mr. Roszak expounds, "they get *into* things, turning every experience into a study, from death, divorce, and taxes to straightening up their desks." That explains Eli pondering the new orchard fence for months. His calculation sheets mount high, whereas I would have had the posts knocked in, in a morning and the cross planks within the week. Of course, I may have had to fudge a little, but a deer-proof fence would have been there within a fortnight. It is actually two years now since the trees were felled for the new orchard and Eli has got the basic fence up, along with the artistic finials on each of the fence posts and has built two of the three gates needed. Not fully gated yet, however, means the orchard is not fully deer-proof, and so, while Eli does more 'workshopping,' I am still awaiting the fruit tree blossom that I thought might brighten my life this spring. "I will die before you get finished, and some other woman will benefit from the new orchard," I tell him. "Be generous," he replies.

Reading all these books reminds me that baby boomers are not team players. They are (or were) all about doing their own thing their own way. (Remember Frankie's recording of "My Way"?) Eli tries to share household chores, but a little distraction and he's back dreaming of the final gate he is going to make in order for the orchard to be one hundred per cent deer-proof one day. He would like to be on our team, but he keeps wandering out on to the field on his own. The following doesn't apply to Eli at all, but I do love Marilyn French's comment on the boomers, "one really charming quality of the narcissistic younger generation is their distractibility; you can easily deflect any unwanted attention they may direct at you simply by asking them about themselves."

A Roper/Age Wave survey showed that boomers put power, wealth and influence way below "being true to myself," not selling out and aiming for inner satisfaction. Certainly this explains some of Eli's behavioural direction, which I unwittingly and with no apparent good reason have always put down to self-centredness.

Boomers

Despite Newton
on his lonely path
and Galileo, forced to kneel,
and Bruno, burned at the stake,
the boomers still believe
the world revolves around them.

The boomers, the boomers, make room for the boomers.

They speak only of
their dogs, and cats,
and children, and fire insurance, and...
everything as though things
were an extension of themselves,
like a kind of Canadarm,
all things only being relevant
in respect to their own daily spinning.

The boomers, the boomers, make room for the boomers.

Give them a good Zen slap
on the side of the head,
so their eyeballs turn to
look outwards for a change,
and their ears unplug
from their own constant voices.

The boomers, the boomers, make room for the boomers.

And when it's done, how
they will shake to find
there's another maypole
around which the world turns
that has little to do with them.

The boomers, the boomers, will there ever be enough room
for the boomers?

Too Late for Solutions?

Before I take a look at possible solutions to the boomer problem, I would like to quote from a paragraph by Machiavelli. What, you may well ask, is a personal essayist and poet of domesticity reading Machiavelli for? Well it happened this way. While over on Vancouver Island for a day's chores, I decided at the last minute to drop by one of the second-hand bookshops in Nanaimo to pick up a copy of Montaigne's essays that I fancied rereading. In my rush not to miss the ferry back to Gabriola, I picked up the book, paid and made haste to the ferry docks. As our car was loading, I glanced in the bag at my purchase and found I had bought Bernard Crick's edition of Machiavelli's *The Discourses* by mistake. Well they both begin with an *M*, don't they? A perfectly understandable mistake to be made by a speedy eighty-year-old. Loath to waste five dollars, I started in on the discourses and found them so relevant to the present political situation in the world that I took to reading them while listening to the *CBC News*.

The relevant passage for the boomers disaster? Machiavelli advises that if a problem is not foreseen and dealt with in its early stages (as the problems arising from the swell of births sixty-five years ago has not been provided for), it is better to temporize than take drastic action that may very well worsen the situation than improve it. If one temporizes, Machiavelli suggests, "either the trouble disappears of its own accord or at least disaster is postponed for a considerable time." Our present government seems to have chosen to temporize as there appears to be no cohesive policy to deal with the shortage of gerontology doctors and nurses, no strategies for what will be a burdensome number of Alzheimer's cases, or plans to increase the number of home care workers, or for the providing of relief for families who are looking after their own frail relatives in their own homes.

Surely there are some wise folks somewhere in power who are gnawing over solutions to the immediate problems of the possible breakdown of our social security system, health care system and pension funding; who are worrying whether there will be an adequate supply of retirement accommodations, nursing homes and hospital beds. Surely there are some caring people somewhere who are working out how to readjust government resources to meet the needs of the burgeoning aged without depriving children and younger people? Aren't there some experienced administrators somewhere who can harness the increasing "grey power" to set things on a more even keel?

Some think the solution to boomers' pensions will be solved by printing money. That is no solution at all, for it merely devalues money and everyone will be worse off. So let's look at some more realistic ideas.

Possible solutions that I've gathered from my reading begin with removing sixty-five as any kind of a marker for retirement. That costs little to do, and sixty-five is an almost arbitrary age that was introduced by Prince Otto von Bismarck when he brought in the first pensions (for war veterans), very reluctantly. He asked, "How old are they when they die?" When told "around sixty-five," he decided to settle on that age to start pensions. It does seem as though "retirement" will inevitably become an obsolete term anyway, since personal retirement savings are dwindling, with one third of all Canadians stating they don't have any at all. Boomers, it seems, prefer to take on debt rather than save and so some of them will be part of the first generation to enter retirement owing money, and will have to consider continuing working. An important aside here is that if firms had better gender balance amongst their employees, that most vulnerable section of older adults, females, would be in a better position to face old age.

The next solution offered in my reading was to foster healthy aging; that is, decreasing the likelihood of multiple illnesses in our old age, by tackling our health procedures at a much earlier age – aging doesn't necessarily mean illness. My sister-in-law, a nurse in intensive care units for many years, explained this to me. "Working in intensive care as I did the majority of my nursing career," she said, "I saw what caused people to be in crisis mode and it was usually years of body neglect. It was rare to see anyone in ICU for medical reasons other than body neglect. Of course, there were accidents causing an otherwise healthy person to require hospitalization, but my overwhelming impression was that people brought disease to themselves by neglecting the basics of taking care of the body."

Another key to answering the boomer problem would be to increase support for and availability of caregivers now; and making elders' roles more productive and integrated into the community. Zalman Schachter-Shalomi says (ever-hopefully and without any supportive evidence) about this situation, "Once elders are restored to positions of leadership, they will function as wisdom-keepers, inspiring us to live by higher values that will help convert our throwaway lifestyle into a more substantial, Earth-cherishing one." Another unreal idealist, I'm afraid. Other more reasonable recommendations are that individuals should plan to adjust their psychological, social and financial expectations (Australians are now compelled to save nearly ten per cent of their incomes by law, why aren't North Americans?) to a new timeline – prepare to possibly retrain at certain times in life, to take sabbaticals for reflection, to be rehired after retirement... That is to look on life more as a cyclical than a linear event; a cycle where one reinvents oneself from time to time. Goals change with age.

As to the younger generation, Paul Samuelson demands that young people become more connected to how they are now and how they will be in the future – a double occupancy of the same body as it were, is what they should plan for. He points out that "giving over goods now to an older man is figuratively giving over goods to *yourself* when old." I wonder if the X, Y and Z generations have considered this. I should mention that most of these suggestions are put forward by Ken Dychtwald, although other authors I've read on the subject provide similar ideas.

Mr. Dychtwald reiterates the need for governments to do several things: to spend more money for research on how to delay, or prevent, the diseases of aging; to train and retrain health care workers as to the specific needs of an aging population (it is called geriatric competency, and few health care workers have it today); to make disease prevention and self-care a national priority; and to orient the economic incentives of our health care system towards healthy aging. On this point he quotes Dr. Walter Bortz who says, "No drug in current or prospective use holds as much promise for sustained health as a lifetime program of physical exercise." Jack Lalanne said, "People don't die of old age, they die of inactivity." He lived to be ninety-six, and so his thoughts on the matter are worth being given some consideration.

All the above aimed at us "living longer, but dying slower" as Mr. Dychtwald so nicely puts it. He also points out that government medical plans were primarily meant to help those who couldn't afford medical care and that people who can afford to pay their own medical care shouldn't be benefiting from them. The last is another example of the misuse of grey power.

Just read a piece by lawyer Sanford R. Altman, Esq. (I haven't seen that way of addressing a person since my childhood. How old can this esquire be, I wonder?) In it he states no one in his law firm expects to have to meet a retirement age. He adds, "Although I am a lawyer and not a mathematician, staying healthy, paying taxes longer and waiting to collect Social Security, along with consuming more as we go, may well give us the huge economic boost we need instead of the drain that many fear." Well, being a wabi-sabi sort of person myself, I don't know about the "consuming more as we go" bit, but otherwise, if he represents the general opinion of the legal profession, there may be constructive thought coming from that section. A good start, I would think.

As a proponent of the position that solutions for all problems start with the individual, I suggest we all look at our own "grey power." By empowering ourselves, by evaluating our talents and using them for the benefit of the community, we are taking the first small steps to closing both the generation gap and the rich-poor one. Once we are self-empowered, linking up with others can only bring solutions closer.

These books I have been reading request you stop thinking of retirement as an extended vacation, but plan how you can use your skills and experience to benefit your community. As Dychtwald puts it "old age should ideally be a time of continued growth, generosity, wisdom, and love." Well there you go, boomers. Read some of these tremendously important books yourself (check the bibliography at the end of this book for a list) and see how your life needs nudging so that its lengthening is supported and enriched by your contribution.

Who'll Go First

A friend told me the following story about her aging parents. Her father had done very well materially in life and her parents lived in high style with a fairly involved life both socially and with their worldly possessions. One day her father asked her mother to come into the library. He requested she sit down and then told her that, should he die before her, there were a large number of things she needed to know how to handle. She gave a little sigh, already exhausted at the thought of having to deal with the complexities that rich people apparently have to deal with. The father started by showing the stocks and bonds that needed following, the various bank accounts and safety deposits. He then moved on to things in the household that needed yearly attention, if not more frequent – the furnace, the gutters, the water filtration set-up, the periodic checkup of their cars. The list seemed endless and even though people would be employed to help in these matters, the mother felt waves of hopelessness sweeping over her. Since she was well-mannered, kindly and loved her spouse dearly, she merely nodded and smiled gently as the lists unfurled.

At the end she gave a long sigh and declared that there was no way she could, there was no way she would, deal with all of that and that she would go first. And that is just what happened. I don't mean to say she decided to die first, and took action on that decision; it was just the way it unfolded.

Even though our life in our little vinyl-sided cottage is so much simpler, I think I would, if I could choose to, prefer to go first. I think all of us, if we are at all honest, imagine, from time to time, what it would be like to have to live without our partner (assuming we have one). It's not just the idea of having to accompany a possibly bedridden companion through their last days, nor the waiting to hear the last breath (as another acquaintance of mine told me how night after night she lay in bed listening to the laboured breathing of her husband, wondering whether the next breath would be the last), it's the thought of having to deal with all the stuff accumulated in a lifetime that bothers.

I am good with garage sales and if I gave a number of those, it would clear quite a bit of the house, I know, but how to maintain the rest? What to do when the computer breaks down? My husband is always at hand to kick mine when needed. Will I have to kick it myself? What to do about door hinges loose, drawers stuck, stove fans stalling...

It's not that I don't have some manual skills. I can handle tools, although electric ones are challenging. It's just that I'm an in-between. An in-between in that I was born when women were still supported by their husbands. By the time the Second World War had started, I firmly knew my path was to acquire a husband, a fur coat, a house and children – in that order. That was the model in the house where I was brought up, and in all the households around us. Even though my mother had been in business, and had once owned her own shop and a couple of houses, that was far in the past and the loss sunk deep in resentment within my mother's ample body.

The Second World War demanded women work, as their men departed for the front lines, and after that, women never looked back. The glass ceiling can be wherever it is today, but in my childhood such a ceiling could barely be conceived of, as it was the rare woman who appeared in politics, in the professions or in serious business. I was brought up to get a degree, it is true, but if not for teaching, it would have to be for social work or some other caring profession. This was irrespective of the fact that the only things I cared about were words and cartoons, for already I knew that something, anything, that made my parents smile could ward off whole days of tempers and sulking.

I married in stockings with straight seams, a hat and lace gloves. I was expected to go – but not to go too far – up the ladder of success; perhaps up just a few rungs until the babies started coming. I guess one is always an in-between, but leaping the chasm from my parents' comparatively inhibited generation to the sexually liberated one was, for me, a large leap that cost me my first marriage.

I doubt there will be any more major leaps in my life, until the final one, but one can never tell. Does one get less flexible as one ages? The comfort of routine perhaps does make us resistant to change. I resist technological changes, but not aggressively so. I have no TV, no cell phone and no microwave. I have done without Facebook and Twitter and managed fine, so I am not likely to adopt those methods of communication when I find poetry is such a wonderful way to tell the world what I want to tell it, in the way I want to tell it.

Life is complex and I think, even as I age, I have developed techniques for living great chunks of it perfectly satisfactorily. The parts I can't cope with I just let fall by the wayside, with no feeling of failure. You may be able to juggle more parts of your life than I can and keep all those balls in the air at once. If you can, I am agog with admiration for you. For me, the less I need to do, or have, in order to survive creatively and keep these words flowing, the less I will do – or have. I don't think these musings have helped me much to create strategies should I become a widow. I am probably not facing it head-on and, yet once again, hope that it is me who will go first.

Pretending

I am sitting in a hot bath,
when, from nowhere, I say to him,
"One of us will die first."
"Yes," he replied, "I was
thinking just that as I read
of the death of Darwin's daughter.
I wanted to rush out into
the garden and give you a kiss,
but I thought you would be having
a good time and didn't want
to disturb you."
"Yes, I was," I reply.
"I was pruning away like
someone possessed and feeling

like it was a purification.
I would have hated to think
about death at that moment.
I wasn't ready." I add,
"I don't want us to die."
He leans over the bath to kiss
my upturned face and we both smile.
We know it is inevitable
and that we are just foolish children
pretending for a moment
that it will never happen.

In Relationship to Another Generation

I still occasionally say "the bee's knees" when I'm speaking of something very good. That phrase arose in the 1920s and nowadays folks might say "cool," "chillin," or "sweet." Eli, being less slangy in his vocabulary than I, uses the word "excellent." That perhaps is a good example of any intergenerational problems we have had; problems because, as I have mentioned, I am a child of the Depression era and Eli, a baby boomer. At the time we got together, I was around forty and he was in his late twenties. "Cradle-snatcher" was the phrase used then. "Cougar," which is sometimes heard nowadays, has a similar disparaging tone, implying some kind of deficiency on the part of one, or the other, or indeed both folks involved. However, our relationship is into its thirty-seventh year, so "deficient" may not be the right word to use for us. We do, however, admit to a bit of a problem in word usage, increased by the fact that my husband was born American and is not familiar with my English clichés. For example, when I might very occasionally use the phrase that "someone is not out of the top drawer," Eli thinks this must be referring to their socks or underwear, whereas I am still showing remnants of the class divisions so prevalent in my early years when I was living in England.

The other problem that our age difference produces is in listening to music. I was a fan of Bing, and of Sinatra (well less so in recent years since I have learned of Frank's Mafia associations, but that has really no bearing on his voice). Eli is an Everly Brothers, Simon and Garfunkel, The Mamas and the Papas, Elvis and The Beatles generation kind of listener. As with all problems, couples who have decided to hang in together usually can find a compromise, and we did for this one. For going to sleep we can now tune into a golden oldies station that covers seventy years of favorites, thus incorporating both our tastes in light music. Actually it is rather romantic as Eli, lying beside me, sings along with the songs of his teens. I can hear when he has chosen one to sing, because it starts with a purring vibration in his spine that conveys to me (since I am snuggled against him), more strongly than words, that memories are flooding in and total word recall is about to appear. Oddly enough, though sex is still in the picture, it is these moments of Eli singing away that endear him to me the most. His pitch may be slightly off, but his heart is strong and true.

A little aside, but younger folk do seem to think that sex stops at fifty, don't they? When I was seventy-nine, I published a book of my poetry called *Sex After 70*. At the launch, one of our many outspoken Gabriola residents had the nerve to ask me whether the book was fiction. Quickly I responded that it was not fiction and that if he was lucky enough to still be around the next year he might be able to read its sequel, "Sex after 80." Dr. Stephen Holzapfel comments, "Sexuality is not an on/off switch. It's a dimmer switch that each couple needs to set at the right level for them – it might not be set as bright as it once was, but it can still provide a warm intimate glow." Though lacking in details, I found this comment rather touching and companionable.

In return for Eli's bedroom serenades, while he is excruciatingly slowly munching his breakfast, I might choose to play music hall songs from the early twentieth century on my keyboard, or my own favorites from the thirties and forties. As Eli comes upstairs to clean his teeth, he might bend down and kiss my neck at such times and thank me for practicing so hard at the piano when I was a little girl. For him that is almost expressing adoration.

> *he stands behind me*
> *as I play Schubert's dances,*
> *hands on my shoulders...*
> *"it makes me so sad," he says,*
> *both our eyes brim with tears*

As we age, our age difference narrows – have I worn him out? Has he kept me young? Growing old together as couples, women, it is said, become more masculine – women become more assertive and less nurturing; men, on the other hand, become more feminine – more nurturing and less aggressive, so maybe this should be taken into account as our temperamental differences seem to narrow. Betty Friedan expounds on this in her immense book *The Fountain of Age*. She felt that the later years are a time for the male to be released from his macho image. If so, perhaps men will be more likely to seek health advice earlier than they do now, and so raise their lifespan to equal that of women. She feels the macho demands of testosterone have cost men a lot. Men should not, she thinks, be threatened by their declining sexual powers but embrace their "feminization," their ability to nourish and care, that has lain so dormant in our macho-demanding culture.

Well I don't know about all this, but I have noticed that when it comes to energy, Eli's speed of doing things, always slower than a snail's, has grown even slower, whilst my speedy behaviour approaches bullet-train speed as I approach tasks with short stretches of colossal energy, before collapsing in true operatic style.

I remember finding an odd book in one of the houses of my childhood which showed how owners looked more and more like their pets the longer they were together. As I always think (not being a pet person myself) that pets represent an unspoken part of the owner's psyche anyway, this piece of information doesn't surprise me. Maybe it's true of couples too.

So as our hormone levels change and our household duties are more and more shared, the fourteen year age difference between Eli and I has closed in until we are just two people being together as best we can, and who can ask more for one's later years?

When I look at Old Men

These days, when I look at old men,
I can only see them young –
the skin clear and sun-burnished,
the back straight, flat belly
and legs firm. Their eyes
shy with curiosity for breasts
and buttocks and the general
wonder of what a woman can be.
I try to see the haired nostrils and ears,
to hear the cigarette-rasped voice,
smell the faint sourness
of the uncared-for, but all
that I vision are young men
bouncing a ball back and forth
over a net on the endless beach,
and young men bragging, or not bragging,
while they furtively graze the crowd,
searching for someone, anyone,
to lead them into manhood, and
distant places, and pushing adventures,
not knowing quite what they are seeking,
but eager to go anyway.

Throw Away Old People Mountain

In past ages when folks got too old to do productive work they might happily be moved to the cottage next door to their family home, so that their children could occupy the main house and keep an eye on them, or not so happily, to some kind of nursing home, or worse yet, to the workhouse. It has also not been unknown in various cultures for "useless" elders to voluntarily, or not so voluntarily, remove themselves from their families who are finding it too hard to provide for that extra mouth.

There is a legend in Japan called "Obasute-yama," or "Throw Away Old People Mountain." Japanese loyalists deny it ever happened, but as similar legends occur among the Inuit and in Germany, Romania, Serbia, Macedonia and East Africa, in fact in most countries that have experienced famine from time to time, it seems unlikely that there is not some truth to the legend. Even in California during the thirties Depression, it was reported that a disproportionate number of grandparents were committing suicide so as to not burden their children. Tales of the throwing away of old people haunted me even before my years of living in Japan. They raise the question of the value of the elderly and their oral tradition in these days of tweeting, and so, feeling that the story I came across in Japan is relevant to Dr. Brogden's book on geronticide that I had recently read, I include my version of it here.

Mukashi, mukashi (for that is how all good stories begin in Japan), a young boy called Taro and his *obaasan* lived together in a small village. He loved his grandmother dearly because she had looked after him ever since his parents had died when he was a baby. Now the village was controlled by a *daimyō*, a warlord. He was a hard-hearted man and, since the area was experiencing a bad harvest and many people were hungry, he proclaimed that all the old people in the village should be taken up the nearby mountain and left there to die. "It is important to feed young people," he said. "Young people can work hard in the fields. Old people cannot work and therefore they should be sent away."

When Taro heard this he was very sad. He loved to have his grandmother take breakfast with him in the morning before he left to work in the fields and he loved to talk over the day with her as they ate supper at the *kotatsu* in the evening when he returned. What should he do? If he disobeyed his warlord, he would be killed, but if he obeyed him, his grandmother would be left on the mountain and would surely die. Taro decided to hide his grandmother. He dug a deep hole in the floor of their hut, and set a futon in it for her to sleep on. He put some food and drink in the hole so that she would have something to nourish her during the day when he was away. He helped his grandmother climb down into the hole and made her as comfortable as possible. Then he covered the hole with boards.

The very next day on the way to his fields, he passed through the village and there on the notice board was a large notice. Taro was not able to read it, for he had never learned, so he asked a priest, who happened to be passing by, what the notice said. The priest replied that it was from their warlord and stated that a neighbouring warlord was going to invade their land unless they could answer a riddle. The riddle was that they had to tell him how a rope could be made out of ashes. Taro's warlord begged his people to come up with a solution to this problem immediately.

"A rope made of ashes? Well that's not possible," Taro said to himself and the other villagers, too, were shaking their heads. When he got home from the fields that night he cooked his grandmother a meal and handed it down to her.

"Grandmother," he enquired, "how would you make a rope out of ashes?"

"Why that's easy," she replied, "but why do you ask?"

Taro explained about the serious notice on the board and his grandmother immediately told him that he should get a rope, soak it in salt water and then, when it was dry, burn it. Taro did as she instructed and was surprised to see that the rope kept its shape, only now it was made of ashes.

His warlord was overjoyed to receive the solution, and gave Taro a bag of gold. Now the village was saved and could live in peace. But this was not to be, for a few weeks later another notice appeared on the notice board. This time the neighbouring warlord demanded that a thread be passed through a piece of bamboo so crooked that such a task seemed impossible. Again he threatened to invade should an answer not be found.

Again Taro asked his grandmother and once more she came up with a solution. She told Taro to tie a thread to an ant's leg and place the ant at one end of the crooked bamboo. At the other end grandmother said to place some honey. Of course, the ant would want the honey and so would quickly run through the twisted bamboo with the thread.

Again the warlord was happy that Taro had the solution and once more gave him a bag of gold. But yet once more the neighbouring warlord came back with a strange demand. This, he stated, was the very last request that must be satisfied, and if it was not, he would certainly invade the village. This time the neighbouring warlord demanded a drum that played itself. "Please do your best, Taro-*chan*," said his warlord, thinking that Taro himself had thought of the other two solutions. "I'll do my very best," Taro promised. He wondered how on earth his grandmother could solve such a problem.

But when he handed his grandmother her evening food, he found she had an answer to this riddle, too. "It's just so easy," she said. "What you do is take a wasp's nest and build the drum around it. When the wasps find they are trapped inside they will buzz around and make the drum sound as though it is being played."

"Oh grandmother, you are wonderful," said Taro, and he leaned down into the hole and gave her a big hug. Of course the warlord was triumphant and gave Taro a third bag of gold. As he did so, he asked Taro how he had thought up those clever answers. Taro could lie no longer. "It was my grandmother...." he began.

"Your grandmother!" yelled the warlord. "Why, I thought I ordered you to take your grandmother up the mountain along with the other old people!"

"You did, sir." Taro bowed low to the ground, not daring to look at his master who was already drawing his sword. "But I have to tell you that I hid her instead and that it was she who knew the answers to the neighbouring warlord's riddles and it was she who saved the village. And now you may kill me or do what you want with me, but I had to tell you about grandmother."

The warlord stood silently for a moment and then speaking in a quiet voice he made an announcement. "I am ashamed that I made such a stupid order. Our old people are full of valuable knowledge and wisdom. All of you go back up the mountain and bring your loved ones back down to the village. Without Taro's grandmother we would all be dead by now. Surely we can share what little food we have with such wise and useful folks."

Taro rushed home with the news and helped grandmother out of the hole in the ground. He showed her the three bags of gold and they danced around their little hut knowing that, for a while, their future was secure.

Owari[1]

But still, if we weren't forced to climb up that mountain, if we could choose to leave voluntarily, when would we? The other night I went to a concert and one of the artists, though interesting, overran his act by a good fifteen minutes. I had always been instructed to leave an audience wanting more.

---

1   *mukashi, mukashi* = once upon a time
   obaasan = grandmother
   daimyō = warlord
   kotatsu = a table with a heating device underneath it
   chan = affectionate diminutive for a child
   owari = the end

But at what point would that be when it came to ending my own life, I wonder?

American academic, ardent feminist and author of the Amanda Cross mystery series, Carolyn Heilbrun was a blunt woman at all times. When asked about the choice to die, she said, "This harsh question, 'What's the point?,' is judged by some as cruel, unacceptable in our culture. To me, it is a very real question, the question that renders living too long dangerous, lest we live past both the right point and our choice to die." Ms. Heilbrun chose her right point and killed herself without telling anyone, or even leaving a message. She did rather take her husband for granted, I feel, saying earlier in her life, "What would happen should I desert him is—is it not?—his problem, one I doubt he spends much time contemplating; abstract questions have never intrigued him."

As an example of a human being choosing when it is time to go, the person whom I would most like to emulate should I need to, but realize I probably don't have the courage to do so, is Scott Nearing. Scott and his wife, Helen, enormously influenced a generation of organic gardeners and stone-wall builders in the sixties. Eli and I were big fans of their writings and their lifestyle. One day, when Scott was one hundred years old, he came in from the woodshed and said, "I can no longer fulfil my duties." What an amazing man, what integrity and what willpower to fulfil the principles he had set himself. This is how Helen described it, "A month or two before he died he was sitting at table with us at a meal. Watching us eat he said, 'I think I won't eat anymore.' 'Alright,' said I. 'I understand. I think I would do that too. Animals know when to stop. They go off in a corner and leave off food.'"

Oh to be so principled as the pair of them! But should elderly people have to justify their existence by their ability to fulfil household duties? What about taking into account all the years before when they had been working; when they had contributed so much?

Charade

I've exceeded
my biblically allotted
years, yet still
my son has not arrived
to carry me up
throw-away-old-people
mountain, and leave
me there with one last
tender look, reflecting
the one I first gave him
at his birth.
Nor has my daughter
thrown wide the front doors
and pointed me towards
the northern tundra,
myself barely bothering
to cover my old body,
knowing a week at most
would find me gone.
In the meanwhile,
I offer the odd opinion,
hoping they will
find it wise,
and keep busy with
small useful things,
smiling continually
lest they think
I am not still participating
in this charade.

Ageism and Elder Abuse

Ageism shows in the way people speak too loudly and too simply to older people on the blanket assumption that they can't hear well or digest information quickly.

— Ted C. Fishman, *Shock of Gray*

Rest your pen, my silver haired harridan, you're no longer relevant.

— Comment on a *Globe and Mail* column by Margaret Wente

Dr. Robert Schwalbe in his eminently readable book, *Sixty, Sexy, and Successful: A Guide for Aging Male Baby Boomers*, offers Robert Butler's useful definition of "ageism" – "a process of systematic stereotyping of and discrimination against people because they are old.... Old people are categorized as senile, rigid in thought and manner, old-fashioned in morality and skills... Ageism allows the younger generation to see older people as different from themselves, thus they subtly cease to identify with their elders as human beings."

Erdman Palmore, who wrote extensively on ageism, suggested that in our society the elderly are expected to be asexual, intellectually rigid, unproductive, forgetful, happy, enjoy their retirement, invisible, passive and uncomplaining.

In order to deny this, some people over sixty waste endless time and effort trying to prove how sexual, with it and bouncingly happy they are. On the other hand, if we get pulled into accepting the stereotypes there is another danger, for as Robert Butler points out, "Ageism, like all prejudices, influences the self view and behavior of its victims. The elderly tend to adopt negative definitions of themselves and perpetuate the very stereotypes directed against them, thereby reinforcing society's beliefs." Perhaps we need to accept the fact that we are growing older, but reject the negative stereotypes of aging and think positively. Professor Becca Levy found support for this notion in her work which reported that older people lived an average seven and a half years longer if they had a positive view of aging, as opposed to those with a negative view.

It would seem that age discrimination pays economically. It sometimes feels as if the ways to marginalize and exploit old people in the interest of economics are endless. For example, ageism, besides exclusion, includes such things as forced retirement, cutbacks on pension plans, and our invisibility in TV ads. In the fifty plus group we represent fifty per cent of consumer spending, but only ten per cent of targeted advertising market. As Jim Fishman, group publisher for AARP Publications, points out, "When an older person sees a product targeted to a younger person, they're willing to buy it, but young people will not buy a product targeted to [an] older person." Inadequate and substandard suitable housing, home care and nursing homes are other examples of how the economy ignores the elderly. The extreme form of ageism, of course, is geronticide. There is a story by the Grimm brothers in which an old woman is buried alive to prevent her being captured. The buriers chanted, "Creep under, creep under, the world is too sorrowful for you; you can no longer follow the commotion." Chilling words when the disposal of old people by omission is still around today.

Dr. Brogden in his book on the subject, *Geronticide: Killing the Elderly*, quotes the story "Half a Blanket" from *Irish Folktales* edited by Henry Glassie, which should give younger generations pause to think. "A man had a father who had grown too old to do anything but eat and smoke, so the man decided to send him away with nothing but a blanket. 'Just give him half a blanket,' said the man's son from his cradle, 'then I'll have half to give to you when you grow old and I send you away.' Upon hearing this, the man quickly reconsidered and allowed his old father to remain after all."

Of course, *Geronticide* makes for depressing reading. Brogden points out that all societies, from primitive ones to sophisticated modern ones have condoned geronticide; everything from outcasting the aged ritually, to a near-starvation diet in Victorian workhouses, to depriving them of life-sustaining medicine in modern nursing homes. Although these cases were more likely to be death-hastening rather than outright killing, the fact is that the image of a golden age when elders were cherished appears to be a myth. Brogden is a legal man, so everything in his book is well-documented and beyond question, but it does dwell on the disposing of the aged without presenting much of the other side of the equation. He doesn't mention the lengthening of life that has occurred and the many dedicated doctors and nurses and probably decent nursing homes around who are helping to make the aging process as comfortable as possible. Brogden states that it is the old-old that are liminal and therefore most easily desired out of the way; old women in particular. "Ageism, in whatever form, has a continuing history in the disposing of those in the socio-economic periphery."

The people in power decide to whom scarce resources will be allotted and that often means people who might benefit from a procedure, such as the very old, may be denied it in favour of someone younger. Old people are often prevented from being admitted to hospital until they are at death's door. Moreover, rather than placing old people in hospitals where they will be covered by public health insurance, they are often directed to nursing homes where they have to pay, at least partially, themselves. In all these cases, Dr. Brogden points out that age is essentially a social construction and revolves around economics. He raises the curious question as to whether governments would actually welcome a cure for cancer, for example, since it would swell the numbers of citizens requiring pensions. This is a question few would dare to ask.

When there is a shortage of food, housing and medical care, citizens who are less adaptable, unlikely to develop new skills and unable to make a contribution to the community will certainly be marginalized, if not threatened. Another outspoken author, Vladimir Skulachev, suggests that older individuals, no longer able to contribute to their community, often die of stroke, heart attack and cancer. He says this happens because, on being marginalized, they become stressed in physical or emotional ways that promote death by stroke, heart attack and cancer. We may not like these ideas, but we should definitely be willing to consider them.

As people slowly lose control of their bodies and have to depend more and more on other people and machines for care, they become objectified, not only by the caregiver, but by themselves. Dr. Brogden describes this marginalization of the aged so well when he writes of relatives starting to think of the person as "on the way out" and the person then gradually beginning to feel that way about himself or herself too. This may accelerate biological death, he feels. He uses the word "liminality" a lot, describing it as when people are perceived as liabilities to the social group, and points out that once this process is set in motion, it is irreversible!! Since power and esteem is factored into the liminal equation, old men (in a patriarchal society) are at less risk than old women.

As an older person becomes liminalized, they are often treated to baby talk. I myself when introduced to my anaesthetist, before undergoing a mastectomy, asked him what he was using as anaesthetic and was told I would be hit over the head. I blasted him and he then meekly gave me a list of chemicals, none of which I recognized! Luckily, or unluckily, he was diverted from attending me by having to give precedence to the victims of a gigantic emergency car smash-up. By the way, I also consider signs such as "One appointment, one medical problem," which I have seen in doctor's offices, to be a form of ageism. At my age, one tends to have a multiple of things go wrong all at once – our flesh, blood and bones all being connected in various ways. The ten minute medical interview is also ungenerous, as focused attention by a caring person can work wonders, particularly in cases of mild depression which often hit the elderly. I understand the brief time allotted from an overworked GP's position, but know that an extra ten minutes might make a whole lot of difference to the client.

Betty Friedan, the doyenne of feminists, has written that wonderful book that I mentioned earlier, which covers so many aspects of aging, *The Fountain of Age*. The words I chose to remember from this immense tome are a counterbalance to my always looking out for examples of ageism, for they warn me of the danger of promoting the elders' interests at the expense of other ages, for that is just an inverse form of ageism. In trying to gain power for ourselves, we mustn't disenfranchise other age groups.

When it comes to what we can do to counteract ageism, Schwalbe gives some helpful advice when he tells us to "(1) point out examples of age discrimination when they affect you; (2) join and become active in advocacy groups that lobby for the interest of senior citizens; and (3) make your own life a model of productive engagement that will demonstrate by your example that older men [let's include women here] can and do make a contribution to society and should be accorded the status in our society commensurate with their contribution." To all this I add that seniors are as diverse as any other group and they don't all have the same needs, nor are they able to offer the same degree of community involvement. Having said that, it is still important to watch out for articles in the press or on the web that characterize older adults as a "burden" and write a response; you could even form a kind of seniors' watch group to counteract such bias in the media. Do everything you can to make sure seniors, and particularly you yourself, don't become "invisible." But most importantly, take a look at how you are coming to terms with your own aging process. People who can't deal with their own aging positively, usually can't come to terms with others' aging either.

Dr. Brogden praises the Canadian Charter of Rights and Freedoms in that it "embodies a commitment to positive discrimination on behalf of *socially unequal* groups." He feels that throughout, our Charter of Rights and Freedoms is concerned with social equality rather than mere legal equality; elderly groups need positive discriminatory action and the idea of "equal citizenship" is not enough. We all want to live longer, why can't a society be created where the old and old-old are at least given some degree of respect? Canada, it seems is at least taking a small step in the right direction. I glow for a moment in the joy of having chosen a half-decent country to live in.

Of course the other extreme form of ageism, just short of geronticide, is elder abuse. Who remembers that great team of Judy Garland and Mickey Rooney – those kids who could take over a barn and put on a Broadway show in a matter of weeks, with little financial support? Well, the very same Mickey Rooney found himself, at age ninety, reporting to a Senate Special Committee on Aging on how he had been abused by a family member, wasn't allowed to make important decisions about his own welfare and had had funds stolen from him. "I felt trapped, scared, used and frustrated," he declared. He also was afraid to report his case.

I have spoken of such elder abuse elsewhere in this book, but so much evidence has descended onto my desk, that I feel I must devote at least a couple of pages to this disturbing problem. It is not a new phenomenon, but with the bulging population of over sixties, it is becoming one demanding of attention. To define "elder abuse" is difficult, but one could say generally that elder abuse is an action, or a lack of action that harms an elder person in what should be a relationship of trust.

"Trust" is really the operative word here, for most abuse of the elderly is by relations and caregivers, people they depend on. The abuse – which can be mental, emotional, physical or financial – usually occurs in the place where the senior is living.

Abuse is often not a simple case of right and wrong. Firstly, the elderly person may, as a result of illness, have become difficult, paranoid and aggressive, and, so, hard to care for. It is not easy to look after an older person who needs to have a variety of pills at different times, who needs diapering, who may be demanding and abusive themselves, not to mention draining to the finances of the caregiver. Burnout and frustration can so easily shift over into abuse. Secondly, the person abused may not just be difficult because of the factors involved in their aging process and illness, they themselves may just be an unpleasant person. They may have wasted their life in crime, drugs, alcohol, etc., and, in their old age, their destructive behaviour, both past and present, may not encourage a caregiver to have a sympathetic approach to their plight. None of this is an excuse for abuse, although it may make neglect perhaps a little more understandable.

As older folk get frail, not only can they no longer look after themselves, but also they lack the resilience to withstand bullying. Physical abuse is not just such actions as pushing and restraining, but also the inappropriate use of drugs to make the elderly more amenable and sexually inappropriate actions. Emotional abuse can include bullying, blaming, ridiculing and the common one of treating the elderly like children. Financial abuse includes appropriation of the senior's funds without their permission, forging of their signature and just plain stealing. Of course, if the abuser has a drug or alcohol problem that makes dealing with the problem doubly difficult.

All this is so painful to write about, and yet it occurs every day – a grandchild on drugs steals her grandmother's jewellery to pay for her addiction, a son ties his mother to a chair while he goes to work or perhaps an overwhelmed caregiving daughter yells at her father that he is ruining her life. In a recent survey, one in five Canadians said they knew of cases of abuse of the elderly, whether it was the hearing of arguments between them and their caregivers, noticing a sudden impoverishment in their environment, hearing of an unexpected change of a legal will, seeing bruises on their body, not being allowed to see the person, noticing unsanitary conditions where the elderly person is being cared for, or that they are wearing inadequate clothing.

I heard of one recently, myself. A friend of mine is losing her short-term memory. Her husband suddenly became very ill and an ambulance was called to take him to hospital. My friend became confused and upset, as was to be expected. She called her son and daughter-in-law, but no one picked up the phone. Then forgetting she had already called, she called two more times within the next hour. Eventually, when she called for the fourth time, the daughter-in-law picked up the phone and yelled, "Stop calling!" Cruel? No. Unfortunate? Yes. The daughter was dealing with two small rambunctious children and was used to her mother-in-law calling frequently for no good reason. She didn't realize that this time the call needed an urgent response.

What can one do about elder abuse? Mild cases might just arise from an exhausted caregiver. Neena Chappell, a professor at the Centre on Aging, University of Victoria, feels giving more support to caregivers is the key to both cutting costs in the health system and tackling abuse originating from the caregiver's fatigue. If caregivers are given adequate support, patients can be kept in their own homes longer and, as she points out, "homecare is 40–75% cheaper than institutional care." If the caregiver is feeling overwhelmed, they could ask others to share a little in order to give them a break. There may be an adult daycare nearby that can also offer relief. The caregiver needs to stay healthy and stress free in order to cope with a demanding person. They can't afford to get depressed and they need to have their own team of positive people around them to support them in their efforts.

All easily said, but in reality a situation may be much more complex and not so simply resolved. Such encouraging things as "restorative justice," which brings abused and abuser together to see if anything can be worked out between them, are suitable in cases where the abuse is not at a criminal level. In more severe cases, elder abuse is a hidden crime and grossly under-reported.

If you are a senior who may be in need of care shortly, you should remember that you are entitled to be safe; to determine your own affairs (or, if you can no longer handle them adequately, have a trusted person to handle them for you); you should have access to information when you are asked to make decisions; and you have a right to privacy (to come and go as you wish, to keep your door closed, to answer your own mail and to be able to speak privately to people). To this end, you should make sure all your financial affairs are in order now and appoint people who you really trust to look after them should you become unable to do so. You should line up your team of supportive friends, helpful medical workers and family members that you enjoy having around, and make sure you keep in contact with them. Social isolation makes people vulnerable to abuse. You may be embarrassed to report when you are being abused, or be afraid of retaliation, but nevertheless you must report it. Family abuse particularly shouldn't stay in the family. Yes, there is someone you can turn to. In Canada, www.seniors. qc.ca will give you information, or call 1-800-O-Canada (1-800-622-6232) for help.

As a child I had a friend who had a domineering father. I hated to go to their house because the father would bully everyone, particularly his mother-in-law, a frail elderly woman, a recent immigrant, who didn't speak English very well. One day I heard that she had drowned herself in her bath, and, young as I was, I vowed I would never allow myself to be bullied in that way. Of course, bullies and abusers are to be found at every stage of life and I have had my share of encounters with them, but it has been my good luck to have had kindly husbands, considerate children and caring friends. I hope that continues until I'm gone. I can only wish the same for others.

Pushed to the margin

When we've become a number on a chart,
and the word "palliative" is heard
by accident, from some careless attendant,
that's when we become will-o'-the-wisps,
in our skin and yet not within,
people on the way out, yet reluctant
to leave the runway yet.
We know you, too, are ambivalent;
wanting us to stay and yet
also to move on, so that you also can.
What can we do, we nearly ghosts,
yet still humans, who would like
to say "I'm still a mensch" when
we know that all the things
that makes us so are
gradually disappearing?

Retirement and Nursing Homes

Eli and I for a while became hooked on the BBC soap opera *Waiting for God*, which was set in a retirement home. It wasn't until I started reading about retirement and nursing homes, in preparation for this book, that I could suddenly see certain things in the show more clearly, such as the fact that the bottom line in private retirement and nursing homes is the money going to the shareholders, the people who really control the running of, in this case, the Bayview Retirement Home.

The retirement homes I have visited have all seemed rather nice (and expensive) if one had no other choice. One of my friends has just had several mild strokes. Her doctor recommended that she shouldn't live alone, and so she has chosen to move into a retirement home. It is luxurious and in no way resembles the retirement home into which I might be obliged to move. The carpets in the corridor are thick and the pictures on the corridor walls are plentiful and non-threatening. I glimpse one of my favourite paintings, Millet's *The Gleaners*, and although it is of peasants gleaning the fields after the harvest, the tones are muted and their poverty is not too apparent.

Her suite is small, and I am at once envious and pitying – neither good qualities to hold. I envy her that she now must live in somewhat simplicity compared to the large condo she came from and must therefore select her most meaningful possessions to have with her in the retirement home. How I would love to be forced to discard half my clothes and at least two or three of my books. Pitying because she doesn't have a garden to float around in, or in my case, wear oneself out weeding in, and even if she had a piano, she couldn't play loudly at any time of the day or night as I can.

On leaving, I accompany her as far as the dining room and again the envy and pitying clash in my head and heart. I am envious of her in that she doesn't have to prepare two large and carefully cooked meals a day as I do, but can sit in leisure, dressed and coiffured carefully, as I notice all the other residents seem to be, at the damask-linen-covered tables. Apart from the grey hair and bald heads, I suppose this could be any fine dining room in a country club. I pity her because she couldn't have veggies straight from the garden as we can part of the year, nor eat piles of fresh fruit straight from the trees and bushes, as we also are able to do, though maybe a little unripe due to our annual race with the raccoons.

Actually the dining room did remind me a lot of *Waiting for God*, in which the characters, Tom and Diana, survive in style in a similar retirement home. Would I organize a revolt as Diana and Tom did from time to time, were I to live in such surroundings? I would probably be demanding that organic fruit and vegetables be served, and a bigger variety of foods be on the menu, or maybe I would protest the hours when the outside doors are locked. But what is there to revolt about, really? Here the surroundings are landscaped, there is no graffiti in sight, the smell is of comfortable bank balances and not urine...such a retirement home is merely a medium luxury hotel with a little more attention than one usually gets in hotels.

Oddly enough it is the retirement apartment block of another friend's mother that attracts me more. It is a large, old apartment building that has been converted into suites. My friend's mother has a bachelor suite consisting of one room and a bathroom. If my first friend in the luxurious retirement home has had to downsize, in this case, my second friend's mother had to very, very much downsize. Here are her truly basic needs – a few treasured pictures on the wall, family photos on the small desk, a quilt from the past on the daybed. What I liked most in this old building was that the very top floor looked out onto the coastal mountains, an eyrie as it were. Here there is a library, billiard tables, Ping-Pong tables and a coffee bar, and it is lively with lots of from-the-belly-out-loud kind of laughter. I could certainly not picture that in the luxurious lakeside especially-built-for-retirement apartments that I had earlier visited. Although this apartment tower is almost touching the clouds, this kind of retirement situation seems closer to the street, the daily give-and-take...and closer to my heart.

The upper apartments here are subsidized housing for the elderly who can manage fine on their own, but think a protective environment, where meals are held in a common dining room and various forms of activity are provided in-house, is just what they need. Many of the residents in the upper floors go south in the winter knowing their apartments will be somewhat secure. Below them are smaller apartments for singles and for those needing to be checked on a few times a day, and below that, rooms for those needing full-time nursing care. It all seems the best one could get in a faulty world.

When it comes to many nursing homes, however, the reports are shocking. Reading the investigations of CBS reporter Vince Gonzales is blood chilling. Betty Friedan, in her ten years of research into aging for her book, *The Fountain of Age*, never faltered from the view that nursing homes were death sentences. Apparently over twenty per cent of nursing homes in North America are understaffed, and what staff there is, is usually underpaid and under-equipped, or guilty of violation towards their clients (one third of the nursing homes in California are apparently involved in such violations). The twenty per cent, inadequately staffed nursing homes cause eighty per cent of the problems. A report declares how the "inmates" would be better off in jail, for in jail there is access to showers daily; constant video monitoring; help when inmates call for it; fresh linen twice a week; access to a library; private, secure rooms; an exercise yard; access to PC, TV and radio; a strict set of rules for guards and a board to take complaints to. Many of these items are apparently lacking in nursing homes. This is a terrible indictment of government inspection. Even in expensive nursing homes, staff shortages mean patients are shortchanged. Laura Watts, outgoing director of the Canadian Centre for Elder Law, commented on the drugging of difficult patients in nursing homes; "This is happening as an epidemic across the country, and it has to stop. We would never accept drugging people with developmental disabilities, and what we are now doing is drugging our senior population into submission."

Another friend reported that her mother fell out of bed and lay all night on the floor before anyone came to check on her; and this in the most expensive nursing home available in the town in which it was situated. "Elder abuse is fast becoming one of the greatest law enforcement challenges," said Paul Hodge, who investigates crimes against the elderly. One of the main troubles, as I mentioned above, is that private nursing homes (and a few chains control the bulk of the market) are answerable to their shareholders, so the bottom line is profit. This is amusingly shown in *Waiting for God*, but the reality is not quite so witty. As Gary Rotstein states, "In the typical American nursing home, too many residents are waiting too long for too little assistance on the good days. And on the bad days, something tragic happens."

The *Toronto Star* ran a series of articles on nursing home abuse that makes horrific reading. Among the complaints were those of people being left in soiled diapers for hours on end, filthy kitchen conditions, the serving of cheap processed food, the cashing of a dead woman's cheque, etc., etc.

Yet nursing homes seem inevitable as baby boomers are frazzled with working full-time, preparing for their own retirement as well as still possibly supporting their offspring at college. They don't also have the energy to care for their parents either in the parents' home, or in their own. But nursing homes are the last place anyone really wants to be, although close to two million people already live in them in North America. Many folk are reported as saying they would rather die than go into a nursing home; a rather ironic comment. Apart from the fears of what an unknown nursing home might present, it is, I think, reasonable to want to stay in one's own home. One's home contains memories, one's creative expression in choice of furnishings and pictures, the familiarity of routine – checking if the morning paper has been delivered, for example. Small routines are still possible for the old-old and keep them focused and interested. Just looking out the windows onto familiar territory is a healing thing.

Reading a report in Dr. Brogden's book, it is scary to note that seven chains of nursing homes receive twenty per cent of the government support of all such homes in the US. Two chains alone have an income of three billion dollars each. Of course their profits depend on laying off of staff members, cutting wages and doubling patient loads. Canada seems to have a couple of chains of its own. Depressing? Of course it is, but depression is overcome by the release of energy and here that energy might well be directed to investigating what accommodation is available for the elderly in your community, and, if it is insufficient, how that could be changed. Here on our little island of Gabriola we have a committee doing just that, and for that I am both supportive and thankful.

If you have time to only read one book on nursing homes, make it *Nasty, Brutish, and Long: Adventures in Old Age and the World of Eldercare* by Dr. Ira Rosofsky. This is at once a bouncingly insightful, depressingly critical account by a psychologist who spends his days assessing residents in nursing homes. I'm surprised he still has a job, he is so frank and devastatingly honest about everything he sees, hears and smells.

From his book, I gather that one third of people between the ages of seventy-five and eighty-four are in nursing homes and that this increases to one half after eighty-four. He states that although nursing home residents may appear superfluous, unproductive or parasitical to some, they actually support a one hundred fifteen billion dollar business. These sidelined folk no longer have the choice of living in public or living in private as we have, they live only in public as their doors are kept continually open. Commenting on the poor quality of the nursing homes and the services they provide, Dr. Rosofsky tells the story of the astronaut who when asked whether he ever gets scared on the launch pad replied, "No more scared than anyone would be sitting on a billion parts all built by the lowest bidder." For those of us approaching nursing home age, that is a scary parallel.

Brogden calls private institutional care facilities "the approved organizational waste-bins for the aged." He goes on to condemn the modern care home by saying "it contains through isolation and reduces through orderly procedures, the disturbance and disruption that are associated with the death crisis." He lists their features – entry rituals that strip identity, a command/obey environment created, people treated as residents rather than individuals, violation of privacy, staff governed by organizational needs rather than individual care... The list is dismal and seemingly endless.

It must be such a difficult decision when an adult child has to put a parent into a nursing home. The subject needs to be approached in a timely manner and not by a herd of offspring, which may make the parent in question feel as if they are being rounded-up and readied for slaughter. I guess that, for the adult children, telling of their own concerns and listening carefully to their parent's responses is the way to go. All changes, whether good or bad, are traumatic and so one's parent may very well feel angry, or worse yet, sad and unwanted. Still one shouldn't feel guilty if the move means an optimum quality of life for everyone – the parent getting the care they need, and the children and grandchildren being able to develop their own lives while incorporating as much care-time as they can for the person going into the home. Caring weekly visits are better than overtaxed attempts at home care when one may not have the necessary skills, and if the attention given to the parent means large sacrifices on the part of the rest of the family when it comes to having carefree time together.

It did make me pause to think about the whole nursing home question, however, when I read Brogden's support of Paul Hodge's accusations. He points out that "care and nursing homes are criminogenic contexts" and gives examples of fraud; physical violence; misuse of restraints; drugs administered for compliance; physical, medical and emotional neglect; and personal property abuse. Well, I had already read that in the top ten ranking nursing homes in the States eleven per cent of the patients had bedsores, seven per cent were confined or restrained and three per cent were in pain, so on reading that nursing homes should be considered criminogenic centres, I immediately called my husband and promised him urgently that I will never, never put him in a home should he deteriorate faster than I. Being, as usual, immersed in a sculpture problem, he seemed a little bewildered at my words, but could see that a similar statement was needed from him, and so he complied.

Music Hour at Sunset Lodge

"You die!"
"No, you die!"
"No, you die!"
The nonagenarian couple
fondly call to each other
in their room
down the corridor,
while I pound out
old vaudeville songs
on an unwilling piano.
The others gather round,
strapped to their chairs,
leaning on their walkers.
They cry out the occasional phrase
as the music jogs their memories
into gear.
"It's a long way to Tip..."
"Hang out the washing..."
"By the light of the silvery..."
"She's only a bird..."
Their voices falter and I,
suddenly aware the piano
seat is soaked from a previous
occupant, hastily rise,
close the lid, and smiling around
in a vague benediction, flee.

Care-ful

I encourage everyone to be an advocate for reasonable humane care of frail older people at home. Advocacy can take many forms, depending on who you are. Frail older people and their caregivers can ask politely for, and insist on if necessary, multidisciplinary healthcare delivered at home, with help available 24 hours a day and seven days a week. If you are a health professional, be aware that this kind of care is considered state-of-the-art for frail people, and you might want to refer clients to such a program if there is one in your community, join one if it makes sense for you, and ask local administrators to consider starting one if necessary. Everyone concerned with aging and good care should try to spread the idea that comfort and function are reasonable and legitimate priorities for frail older people who choose them, and the default when those kinds of people have problems at home should be good professional care where they live, not a trip to the hospital.

– Dr. John Sloan, in response to a query by the author

I'm starting this chapter with a long quote from Dr. John Sloan, to whom I am dedicating this book. He is the rare doctor who does home visits to the very frail and elderly. It is not the dramatic role of the surgeon, or that of the miraculous specialists who save lives regularly. It is the day-to-day plod that cannot result in a return to health for the person visited, but can result in them being given loving attention and being offered the best support available.

Most people who are retired live either by themselves or in nursing homes via retirement homes; few live with their family as they once did. Families are smaller, and what children there are that could offer care to the elderly often live further and further away from their parents and so are less and less likely to be able to offer regular support.

A woman died recently on our island at a very ripe old age. She had lived alone in her last years, but had a caregiver coming in everyday to see how she was doing. She also had a team of visitors. I was not part of that team. I myself would hate knowing that on Monday, J. would be visiting me, and on Tuesday, M. It takes energy to have visitors and I, being a person who lives a large per cent of the time inside my head, wouldn't have the energy to keep them entertained. Of course, they would be supposed to be caring for me, but it doesn't always work that way.

"She gets very sad and cries," someone told me, after a visit, and I responded, rather callously it must sound, "Who doesn't?" Awareness that we all die alone is one of the truths I have gotten used to as I age, but I must have known it earlier, for when I first met him, I asked my present husband whether he would stay with me until I died, an unusual thing to ask for, and hardly romantic, but essentially a survivalist's request. Caring for a person can be a way of controlling them, and being provided with a team of social visitors would be my idea of hell. God (if there is one) spare me the pity of others. Unlike the person I am telling you about, I already do not keep up with worldly matters. I belong to the Thoreau school of thought, for he said, though not perhaps in so many words, one murder is enough to read about, one dog biting a boy, one village scandal. We don't seem to learn much from life, however, and so the endless breakings of the ten commandments and endless committing of the seven deadly sins go on, but having read one example of each, isn't that enough? So when I am old-old, I probably won't want to keep up with worldly events and will continue to let my reading habits and DVD watching float me to wherever my fancy is taking me. It rarely has taken me into the news of the day, so it probably will continue to avoid reality in the future.

Another friend has just moved from a condo into a retirement home where she knows someone will be available should she need medical attention. She has her own apartment in the retirement home and although it is a large downsizing, she is doing it in preference to living with her children. She loves her children dearly and they have been wonderfully supportive of her, still, she is determined to be independent until she can no longer be. I, having a partner, have worked out a pleasant way of survival that the younger generation might well define as codependency. I remember once giving a talk about an experiment my husband and I did, many years before, in living as self-sufficiently as we could – providing as much of our own food as possible, and making as much as we could of the things we wore or needed. At the end of the lecture, a student asked me whether I didn't think that that was a state of codependency, and I replied that if she thought about it carefully enough, she would see that the whole world was codependent. I knew what she meant, however, and now our situation seems even more codependent as I do the social arrangements, cooking, laundry and veggie garden, and Eli does the computers, driving and care of the car, fruit trees, vacuuming and heavy tool work. On the other hand, one could use the milder term "division of labour" and consider my situation very satisfactory.

If I go first, Eli will easily take over the demands of cooking, laundry and social engagements; he will just float into them as they arise. I, on the other hand, would lack a handy man, heavy-duty gardener, chauffeur and lover. It hardly bears thinking of how I would be able to supply these. I'd better show more appreciation and give him an occasional massage when his back is aching.

When it comes to caring for the frail and old-old, middle-aged people often feel guilty if they assist their parents into a care home. I don't feel they should. Loving doesn't mean doing your duty whether you want to or not, or whether you are skilled in that direction or not. It means finding the best care for a parent, or loved one who needs some assistance with their living, although a nursing home may not be the best way to go.

The middle generation, a comparatively new phenomena, have to support their parents at the same time as they are supporting their offspring through college – or later when they fail to leave the nest, or worse still, return to the nest being unemployed. Meanwhile this middle generation have to try to build up their own retirement fund. Those in the old-old group, who might have already died in days gone by, are now still alive, and so demand attention. These middle generationers have become what is known as the "sandwich" generation. It is hard for them not to favour one piece of bread over the other. Families with four living generations are not uncommon these days, and for these, more parents and grandparents need supporting than children. Caregivers, usually women, may have to leave work and careers in order to nurse an elderly, and possibly very sick, relative. This is bound to strain marital relations as there will be no years when empty nesters can have a little more freedom to enjoy life in alternative ways such as travelling together. If you want to read a touching account of a wonderful father explaining to his children why he has to spend time away from them with his ailing mother, read Ken Dychtwald's excellent book *Age Power*.

Are there solutions for the problem of middle generationers supporting the generation before them and the generation after them at the same time? Sharon O'Brien suggests that they get their children to pay for their own education by working, or taking out student loans, and ask their parents to use their own funds to finance their care for as long as they can. Harsh words, but oh so practical.

I should consider Alzheimer's disease here because it, and senile dementia, is going to make enormous demands on care givers in the coming years. By 2040, twelve million people are predicted to have Alzheimer's in the US. Twenty-five to fifty per cent of over eighty-fives already show signs of Alzheimer's, and by 2050 it is forecast that one out of three deaths will be due to dementia. From the onset of symptoms, patients can live eight to ten years with this disease. A cure is nowhere near the horizon, and, as Dr. Guy Brown says, "It is impossible to know what it is like to experience Alzheimer's disease from the inside, or another dementia, or extreme old-age – but it is worth thinking about because that is where we are all headed." At the moment of writing, the Alzheimer Society of Canada was begging the Canadian government to get some comprehensive strategy together to deal with this overwhelming problem.

The Remains of the Day

I need my energy for dying
I cannot spare it
for entertaining folks
coming to see me die;
nor for folks trying to
delay my dying,
with pills and lotions and
various prescriptions.
Nor will I have energy
for folks coming to gloat
that their bodies are still intact,
while mine decays rapidly.
Nor energy to waste
on folks who are going to miss me
too much because they
have invested too much
in having me around.
In fact, any such visitors
would be barely welcomed.
As my days close,
I would like to be lying
in my favourite bed,
with the light filtering in
through gauze curtains
that blow gently in the breeze,
reminding me of the passing seasons.

The Trout Quintet would be playing
in an endless loop on the CD player
and Pride and Prejudice would be running
endlessly on a DVD player, and,
on my bedside table,
The Remains of the Day.

My House for When I'm Really Old

In the interests of avoiding retirement homes or nursing homes when I am old-old, I dream of building a house that will use cutting-edge technology. Such a home is apparently called a "smart" home, but since I haven't been smart about much in my life, the use of that word halts me a little and so I am approaching the whole project with some caution. By cutting-edge, I don't just mean a wheelchair-accessible home with low counters and wheel-in showers. When I say cutting-edge, I mean a home with floors that respond should I fall on them. They'll be electronically attached to a call station that will alert an emergency crew who will immediately respond. I hear "bouncy" floors – a raw egg can bounce on them unbroken – are now available to soften my future falls and, as extra protection, I will, of course, wear hip-protectors to help me bounce back up, should I trip. Such devices are called assistive domotics and they include devices already in use for security and energy conservation. Examples of these are stoves with induction heating that can cook a meal but will never burn a hand; shelves that descend on an hydraulic arm, at the push of a button, so the contents at the back of the cupboard can be reached easily; a bed that monitors bodily functions, and another that can roll a person over to prevent bedsores. As baby boomers threaten to overload the health care system, the government is, a little belatedly, seeking ways to reduce the need for costly nursing homes and health care facilities. They're investing some energy into the research and promotion of just such tools to aid the old-old to stay in their own homes.

Tesla had demonstrated remote control even before the twentieth century began, by startling people with a remote-controlled boat. So the idea of having remote control over things in the house has been around a while. Already gadgets have lightened our load: a lot of food preparation is done in factories; machines wash our clothes and dishes; electricity and gas have simplified our lighting and heating, and thermostats our temperature control. We are used to machines in the home, so how much further can that idea go? However far, I plan to incorporate some of these ideas in my home for when I'm old-old.

Furniture in my home for when I'm really old, and even my clothing, will have micro-devices in them to recognize when I am at risk. I might find it useful to wear a smart shirt to pick up my vital signs and send them to a twenty-four-hour medical centre, which would also store my medical records. This transmitter would somehow not be dependent on batteries. I wonder how such a shirt would be washed.

Security tools, fall prevention devices – did you know that not having loose rugs is probably the biggest fall-prevention action you can take – and automatic timers will all go a long way to alert nearby caregivers. I'm not wild about having video cameras installed; at the moment, I rarely do anything privately that I would be embarrassed for others to see, but I very well may in the future. However, a tracking device that would pinpoint where I am as I move around my new home is fine with me.

My oven will recognize the ingredients in the dish it's cooking and switch off at the right time, thus preventing wastage of food because I was in the garden weeding and became so absorbed that I completely forgot about the meal I had been preparing. I have recently read of a smart trash can which can, by using radio frequency identification antennas, identify objects in the kitchen, thus recognizing items that have been used, or thrown out. This could possibly let my family know if I have lapsed into unusual eating habits such as living on liquorice or Smarties, or have thrown out useful items such as my prescription glasses. Controls are available that can distinguish a dry floor from a wet one, and would be useful should I be unable to deal with burst pipes, taps left on accidentally or flooding from outside rains.

Of course, cameras are already available to tell who is at the door, and I would use a cellphone to let the new arrivals know if they weren't welcome. A remote would let visitors in and lock the door behind them.

In a fire emergency, for people like my husband who have lost their sense of smell, the usual smoke alarm would sound, but also, the lights would flicker wildly and if the danger was extreme the fire department would be alerted.

An automatic reminder system would be a handy addition to my ideal home, connected either to my computer or a loudspeaker system to announce "time for your pills," or "your library books are due." Perhaps it could also turn lights on or off as I enter or leave a room.

Elsewhere in the house, the central computer system will also control lighting, temperature and everything else. I have seen a photograph of a patch panel for just such a system, and it is daunting, but then my robot would take care of the repairs. I might just let Philips do the whole thing with their CarePoint Resident Safety System, although I did nod off to sleep while watching their long and detailed illustration of how it works. Still it would "control and document and print out regular reports" of my status, and for a mild hypochondriac, such as myself, that might make interesting reading. I wonder if I could defibrillate myself with that nice little gadget they have. It is labelled "For the ordinary person in the extraordinary moment," which sounds slightly Zen. Actually the Philips' system is meant for nursing home control, so might be overkill in more than one way for my robot house. Their Lifeline system has helped thousands apparently, so I should be grateful they are working on such systems and not always question their motives.

I recently saw a truly amazing automatic arm that offered a glass of water to a quadriplegic, so, should I get rather feeble, I'm sure there will already be devices to dispense my pills. I hope I will never need a spoon-feeding robot, although it might be welcome in other homes.

A vacuuming robot is already available and, apparently, there are care-providing robot FRIENDs who can help me prepare meals and might even be able to help me meet my writing deadlines. Of course, it will be a long time before such technology will totally replace caregivers, and for those of you ready to rush out and throw money at such devices,

I should warn you that they are meant to help, not replace, caregivers

All these devices would be able to tell when I was home and when I was away and adapt suitably. Since I am an environmentally conscious being, I would have a smart grid to minimize power usage and, of course, it would all be Green Automation to guard against my misuse of community resources.

For amusement, a machine would sense my mood and offer classical music with a touch of country music thrown in. DVDs such as *Pride and Prejudice* (with Colin Firth), *Easy Virtue* (again with Firth) and *Born Yesterday* (with a magnificent performance by Judy Holliday) would run continually. A book reader (should my eyes fail) would entertain me with the very same *Pride and Prejudice*; *84, Charing Cross Road*; *War and Peace*; *The Uncommon Reader* and a few other such titles to keep me in a pleasant mood.

I don't drink coffee, have indoor plants or pets, or an outdoor pool, so, I could at least eliminate electronic controls that would make coffee at a distance, water my plants, walk my pets or clean my pool. For those of you who do and have, I've been told such devices already exist. When it comes to pets, I know that pet robot seals are already available to give tactile comfort to dementia sufferers.

Folks do warn there will be a learning curve to all this, and since I don't even own a cellphone, and have trouble going beyond word processing on my computer, I honestly think mine will be a very steep curve. All these novel aids, while welcome, may be just too much for the uncomplicated life I have established for myself. I know I should be flexible, but my joints tell me this is getting more and more difficult.

So, I think, on due consideration, that when I am old-old, I might just move to the garden shed at the bottom of the yard, where there is just enough room for a bed, with a small table for my yellow writing pads, a jar of yellow pencils and a large shelf for my favourite books. There I will live on bread and cheese and raid our garden when I need veggies or fruit. That appeals to me as a much more reasonable personalized shelter than a robotized house for when I am very old. Thoreau, move over.

Checking Off for Checking Out

My twin, systematic to the point of obsession, has sent me a little book. It is called *LifeBook* and is put out by Age UK. It suggests you make lists of everything you need to do, and practically need to say, in order to prepare for a smooth dying. My twin informs me that filling in the information in the spaces provided in the book is easier than filling out your income tax, and much more fun. *LifeBook* starts with the obvious – your name, address, phone number (and mobile), email and the same for your spouse and next of kin. Then you should list the relevant facts about your offspring and your pets. We are not "pets" people ourselves but appreciate that a dog's special needs should be noted should its owner not be there. Ah! I see close friends are to be listed before your own medical conditions, well you could very well be donating them body parts so it's good they take precedence. Notes on your health and work contacts come next and then home contacts should you be lucky enough to have a maid or gardener. We double duty as both employer and employee in these respects, which, as you may well suspect, is an unsatisfactory arrangement. Ah the milkman, newsagent and greengrocer are listed next...shades of nostalgia for me as the coalman from my childhood comes into view in my mind, with his horse and cart trundling down the back alley behind our house and ready to drop sacks of coal into our coal cellar.

I'm glad to see tradespeople are listed before solicitors, accountants and spiritual leaders. The British are such a practical people. At this stage in the book we come to our records of financial accounts, credit cards and "other regular payments." These pages are edged in a bright cheerful blue, lest we succumb to melancholy at this stage of our entries (if we have not already succumbed to writer's cramp before now). I should mention that the British apparently still do not think it good manners to talk about money, or death directly, so the whole questionnaire handles these matters rather obliquely.

Next you must indicate in the space provided just where you have stored your relevant documents. As Eli and I have lost our wills several times, we now keep them out in public display on the opened dictionary, which sits on its reading stand. Thanks to Google, the dictionary lies open at "opsonize" and is unlikely to have a page turned in the near future, so those wills will stay put, at least for the moment.

Now we come to practical details. Who will act as your power of attorney if your mind conks out before your body and things like that. Then it gets down to actual funeral plans – dealing with possessions and flowers at the funeral and such things. My twin, who has actually filled the whole book in, was rather gleeful about this stage of dealing with possessions, and while she doesn't own a car, she happily listed her million dollar condo under possessions. She also specifically named dealers who should be approached to buy her art and book collections. She is well-known in both the art and book world in London, and would have dealers lining up for some of those rare editions she has, whereas Eli and my books (and we have a fine collection) are mostly marked as library rejects with the library stamp clearly marked on each.

Ruth, my twin, has already planned her funeral down to listing all the people she doesn't want to attend. She has recorded the last song, last lament and epitaph she expects to be sung, read, and inscribed, not to mention the fact she has already written her obituary for the *Times* to at least match, if not outrun in length that of her ex's.

The *LifeBook* finally indicates you might want to leave a last message. Well, I've just sent Ruth and my offspring a CD, about twenty minutes long, of me reading from my best poems and essays, enough to send anyone to pleasant sleep I would think.

As I received *LifeBook* from my twin on my eightieth birthday, I guess she was hinting that I'd better get started with my preparations for dying. In a Scandinavian study it indicates that if Ruth, my identical twin, lives to be ninety-two, I am two-and-a-half times more likely than any random female in the population to do so also. I don't quite know how to read this statistic, so I ponder whether I had better get going filling in the wretched book now, or put it aside because I probably have a couple of year's grace yet. I have come to no conclusion.

I may have made fun of this death-preparation booklet, but it is actually very handy and I should mention that

Age UK, who put out the booklet, also has a great checklist before you choose a nursing home; just enter "care home checklist" and "Age UK" in Google and up it will come. H. H. Dilgo Khyentse Rinpoche asks, "we make strenuous efforts to ensure that in the future we will not run out of money, run out of food, or be without clothes. But of all future events, isn't death the most crucial?" If you want to help your family so that they don't have to make decisions when they are gathered at your bedside, write them down now. If you make your wishes about final medical care and your funeral arrangements clear now, your children will have less anxiety when the time comes.

The Way I See It

In the process of preparing for *A Roller-coaster Ride*, I read over fifty books on aging. The information, both the trivial and the extraordinarily detailed, overwhelmed me. Not only that, but most of them lacked any sign of humour. I don't mean that they should have been filled with a load of "old codger" jokes, but they should at least have offered some wry comments on the human condition that would allow the reader a little light relief from all those ponderous warnings and statistics. I'd like to mention in the connection of aging and humour, that Matt Parker and Timandra Harkness have a witty fringe show on the mathematics of death called *Your Days are Numbered*. You are told you will have a 0.000043 per cent chance of dying during the performance.

Being over-eighty myself, I scanned the medical advice – not just for what to do in emergencies, and how to live to be over a hundred, but how to make a well-considered choice when symptoms become worrying. Overloading oneself with information is not a good way to go about this, so I shredded my stacks of notes, threw them up in the air like a mass of confetti blessings and set out to note down the bits left in my exhausted brain that I must have felt were relevant to my situation. Now I usually only partially chew my facts, and am definitely given to misinterpretation as I seize the odd note here and the odd suggestion there that appeals to me, so you should definitely do your own reading and work out your own path into old age. Mine may be totally inappropriate for you, but, for what it's worth, here it is.

Firstly, on my desk are the following couple of reminders in big print:

> There is not a pill for every ill,
> although there may be an ill for every pill.

And

> People who do not need treatment include:
> people who are not yet ill,
> people who cannot be expected to get well,
> and those for whom doctors have
> not yet any more effective treatment
> than a kind relative might offer.

Now for other advice I recall from my mass of reading:

- If I am spitting quantities of green sputum or blood, or have crushing chest pains, I should get to a doctor immediately (my husband's rule – only go "if the bone is sticking out through the skin"). Otherwise, I should be an informed participant in the medical interventions I might have to choose as I age. This is, of course, impossible, for even doctors in one speciality have scant knowledge of another speciality, so vast is the information available. Google is being used more and more by lay people, to the exasperation of doctors who give more import to their years of training and experience than to a five-minute Google search for what a few strange symptoms might mean. When I had breast cancer, my husband lugged a load of printouts to the surgeon's office. He looked at them with disdain and pronounced, "You two are just too clever for your own booties." This was probably a correct assessment, though at the time we didn't think so.

- Everyone can expect headaches, rashes, creaking joints, insomnia and bowel changes happening from time to time as one ages. I should not rush for medical aid when these occur. They will pass. I should learn to cope with them. If I can't cope, the odds are that something in my personal life – money matters, interpersonal relationships, etc. – is draining me. Coping skills should be adequate to deal with most intermittent body fluctuations.

- I should avoid invasive surgery at all costs – this includes the putting of stents and balloons into arteries that, if inserted, may change the cause of death, but won't extend my life at all. It appears angioplasty, a frequently used procedure which involves pulverizing plaques, creates the possibility of the debris occluding the vessel that caused the heart attack in the first place. I carefully noted Dr. Nortin Hadler's take on unnecessary heart surgery: "Interventional cardiology is what supports almost every hospital in America—it's an enormous part of our gross domestic product. Every year in this country we do about half a million bypass grafts and 650,000 coronary angioplasties, with the mean cost of the procedures ranging from $28,000 to $60,000. There are a lot of people involved in this transfer of wealth. But no Western European nation has such a high rate of those procedures— and their longevity is higher than ours [the US]."

I shouldn't go for back surgery either. I really like Dr. Hadler's take on back pains: "None of the various forms of poking, prodding, injecting, exercising, yanking, girding, needling, and the like can be shown to consistently and robustly offer advantages over placebo events. None of the various pharmaceuticals have effectiveness, efficacy, risk/ benefit ratios, or cost/benefit ratios that exceed that of low doses of aspirin or acetaminophen." All this from a man who has served on endless government investigations and committees.

I should also avoid biopsies, which at the worst shift your cancer cells around in an alarming manner, and at the best change you from the status of "human being" to one of invalid. As I have had a mastectomy, I was very interested to read of the recent change of governmental guidelines on who should have breast screening and who might be harmed by it. False positives set off a string of unnecessary tests and treatments and can cause needless anxiety. This is particularly so for women between forty and forty-nine years old. The researchers also say screening can find cancers that grow so slowly they would never affect a woman in her lifetime. Having had a mastectomy after fourteen biopsies, this advice is a bit too late for me, but did give me pause to wonder about the medical trap of biopsies and lumpectomies I found myself in for four wretched years, some years ago.

- Preventative drugs are taken because of hope. People who take medicines or opt for procedures, have usually no idea if they will do what they claim. Preventive medicine is wasted on the very old anyway, and makes the young into invalids. The pharmaceutical industry is making patients of all of us. An example of this is given by Dr. H. Gilbert when he points out that by lowering the fasting blood sugar count from 140 to 126 (for the definition of diabetes) 1.6 million people suddenly became invalids. With cholesterol-level testing for three-year-olds being suggested, and the possible future genetic testing of newborns being introduced, soon it will be impossible to tell the difference between healthy people and sick people. I agree with Dychtwald that people should take responsibility for healthy living, but there is a difference between that and wholesale hypochondria from kindergarten onwards. For a devastating article on this over-medicalization, please read Alan Cassels, a drug policy researcher, at http://www.newint.org/features/2003/11/05/peddling/.

If you can take a lot of anxiety and stay cool, I can't recommend these books enough for pointing out the hazards of the medicalization of life: Dr. Nortin Hadler's Worried Sick: A Prescription for Health in an Overtreated America; Ray Moynihan and Alan Cassels' Selling Sickness: How the World's Biggest Pharmaceutical Companies are Turning Us All into Patients; and Dr. H. Gilbert Welch's Overdiagnosed: Making People Sick in the Pursuit of Health. Dr. Hadler describes our over-health-consciousness in this way:

> We [the US] are a country of obese,
> hypercholesterolemic, hypertensive, diabetic,
> osteoponic, depressed, pitiful creatures
> perched on the edge of a cliff staring at
> condors: cancer, heart attacks, strokes,

dementia, fractures, and worse. We fear for
our future. We teach our children that they,
too, must live in fear for their futures.... No
infant can simply be fussy, and no child can
simply be fidgety, obstreperous, or below
average in performance. We are told that all
these are symptoms, or at least harbingers,
of disease. We are a vigilant society.

Hadler's thesis is that many healthy individuals
are being thrust into invalid mode by contrived diseases –
a person with just a predicament being pushed over into
becoming a patient with an illness that is pointed out as
possibly life-threatening and therefore demanding unproven
and unnecessary remedies. I feel that by medicalizing
everyone, those who are seriously ill are being trivialized.
Dr. Hadler offers lots of statistics and references in support of
the extreme position he takes. Other medical advice books
are mere band-aids when compared with his book and the
one by Moynihan and Cassels. Such readings will give me
pause for thought in the future before I might rush to my
local island GP, who is a wonderfully caring being by the
way.

The moment my doctor gives a name to my symptoms
I become an invalid...look at it, "in valid." My doctor will
start to treat me like a patient and so will my friends and,
worse yet, I will start to treat myself like one. That is a recipe
for depression. I shouldn't enter the medical therapeutic
envelope without due consideration. I might just get stuck
under the flap. Even if I am diagnosed with an illness, I
don't need to become the illness – don't be a diabetic, be

a person coping with diabetes; don't be an arthritic, be a person dealing with arthritis.

• When it comes to medical bias, as Upton Sinclair said, "It is difficult to get a man to understand something when his salary depends upon his not understanding it." According to Dr. John Sloan, drug companies finance half the research done in the western world. Some of the remedies I am recommended will probably be doing stockholders more good than they will be doing me. And while we are dwelling on the pharmaceutical companies, I am advised to check out which pharmaceutical, or medical technological company has been financing support of research into the drugs and procedures I am contemplating taking and whether the doctors promoting these procedures do, or do not have connections to these companies. I remember once, on having a bladder complaint, being advised by an urologist to take X pills for life. Soon after, good sleuth that I am, I found out that he had shares in the pill-producing company. I stopped taking the pills immediately (a little concerned that I would drop dead without them) and took warm water and lemon every morning as my father used to. After a while I got bored with that and dropped it too. I have never had cystitis since. Of course if doctors are connected with pharmaceutical companies, that doesn't necessarily mean they are biased towards that company's drugs, they may just be concerned that they get the right drug to their patient; but it does give pause for some thought on the consumer's part.

I read that pharmaceutical company tests may well distribute wealth nicely in the healing professions, but will do nothing for me. I should learn to read statistics (for example, there is a big difference between relative improvements caused by a drug and absolute improvements) and see what my odds are. I need to know the benefit/risk of every drug I am offered (or natural cure come to that) and every surgery suggested. This applies even more to invasive treatments which could well introduce iatrogenic illnesses (those caused by medication or hospital procedure), apparently a formidable presence these days. The use of too many tests in our medical system is based on fear of lawsuits for inadequate treatment. No screening being offered? A malpractice suit is on the horizon. Someone rather cynically said that "if you think you are healthy, you just haven't had enough tests." I should check out whether the target population for the tests that underlie the treatment being offered to me is actually similar to my profile. It's no use if the trial was for adolescents, when I am eighty. I should make sure that the studies have been properly carried out without bias, and that the results have been correctly interpreted. All this takes time, but it is my body and so I should invest time. I should also weigh up the cost-benefits of the procedure being offered. For example, I am considering whether to have a crown, or a restoration of a broken tooth. The difference in cost is a thousand dollars. I am eighty and will probably take the gamble that a restoration will last me out. Cost-benefit consideration is why preventive medicine is useless for the very aged because the medicine may take longer to take effect than they'll be alive.

While we are on the subject of pharmaceutical companies and clinical trials, I should quote Dr. John Ioannidis, who has spent his life evaluating trials of drugs. He says adamantly, "Most medical treatment simply isn't backed up by good, quantitative evidence." A disquieting statement, if ever I read one. He found that many studies were followed by others refuting their claims. He thinks that two thirds of published medical research is wrong.

• I am realizing that I am at the mercy of the state of medicine at the time I need it – in the past tonsillectomies, hysterectomies, radical mastectomies (just recently they have begun suggesting not all breast surgeries need remove lymph nodes – almost a standard practice until now), laminectomies (spine surgery to remove a portion of the spine) were all standard procedure. Homosexuality, menopause, puberty and orgasm (the lack of) have all been treated as illnesses at one time or another. I could add that these days, menstruation, baldness, wrinkles, shyness, sneezing and hair loss are all being approached as problems to be dealt with by using newly developed drugs by pharmaceutical companies

• I learned that too many prevention and rescue methods are used with older people when what they really need is to be spoken to calmly about death. When it comes to treating the elderly, most doctors are half-hearted about preventive methods, yet are reluctant to give them up, possibly from fear of litigation. Two per cent of frail people use thirty per cent of the health care budget. How much of this is on useless tests and useless preventative treatment? I should make sure I am not guilty here. I don't want to be using ambulance services, drugs and procedures that could well benefit a younger person far more than they would benefit me. When it comes to treating the very old, the usual guidelines do not apply, for evidence-based medicine, based on trials, only tells probabilities and approximations. Frail older patients are not average they are outliers, folks who need to be considered individually and intuitively. You can't use 'cookbook medicine' with them.

• The last ten years of my life may be tough. I should gather family, friends and community around me...well I should select elements of all these carefully for the support they are willing to offer. Don't go for longevity; go for what allows you independence and comfort. "We're here for a good time. Not a long time," sings the rock band, Trooper.

• I should be aware that there are doctors who do badly what I need doing well (it's called malpractice); doctors who do well what I don't need doing at all (it is called over-medicalization, "meeting the unneed," someone said); and doctors who are caring, listening (for more than ten minutes) knowledgeable beings. I should choose the last. Here's Dr. Hadler's advice on the matter: "I think the patient's job is really to find the right person, the right doctor. You need a relationship with a physician who can listen to your experience of illness and consider with you the benefits and risks of all options. The system is not set up to benefit you in this fashion, because it's set up as part of an enormous business model. There's too much that we're doing that doesn't help. That doesn't mean we don't need physicians, or that many aren't caring people."

• It is recommended that I don't go for new belief systems, new jargon that may go for symptoms, but which doesn't explore the basic causes of discomfort. This can happen in the regular medical situation as much as in the parallel healing professions.

- I shouldn't go for patent medicines that might well be adulterated with pharmaceuticals and heavy metals. Check http://www.mskcc.org/aboutherbs for pluses and minuses of natural cures. My own medicine drawer? It holds some antihistamine for wasp stings, some stuff for foot warts, hydrogen peroxide and rubbing alcohol for cuts, calamine lotion (my childhood cure-all) and a small bottle of Tylenol for house guests with headaches (we never seem to need it). On the shelf I keep a large aloe plant that I cut chunks off for burns. That's it. No prescription drugs, no sleep-inducing pills...nothing else. My rule? Caveat emptor for all ads for prescription drugs, herbal remedies and dietary supplements.

- My general impression from the books I have read is that doctors should return to the road...that is to house calls and the personal comforting that is necessary whether treatment is to follow, or not. When my family was young, our family GP told me that seventy-five per cent of the people who came to see him just needed a friendly ear. A fifteen minute chat in a doctor's office (or preferably in one's own home) could well be worth more than a thousand dollar scan in the hospital.

- I should take responsibility, as far as I can. There is no point in blaming the greedy pharmaceutical companies, the highly paid hospital and health care administrators, the doctors who stick to guidelines for fear of litigation and so tend to treat patients as numbers on a chart rather than individuals. It's up to me to choose my health care team, and to have them of one mind (mine), so that when I need them they will work appropriately with me. I should learn not to be gullible when it comes to advice.

• I should be well-nourished with a balanced diet leaning towards lots of fruit, veggies, nuts and seeds. I know my longevity depends both on my genes and my lifestyle. It seems the new fountain of youth springs from a diet of vegetables and nuts, physical activity, no smoking, a limited alcohol intake, seven to eight hours of sleep a night, no snacking and a normal BMI. Still I read a record not long ago of a certain Javier Pereira, who died in Columbia after being studied at a New York hospital in the 1950s, claiming to be one hundred fifty years old, having been born in 1789. When asked about the secret of his longevity, Pereira said that one must chew cocoa beans, drink plenty of coffee, occasionally smoke a big cigar, and not worry. I may not adopt this recipe, but the choice does seem to be up to you.

Even though fifty per cent of North Americans use supplements, I abstain and put the money into the greengrocery section of the supermarket. I don't smoke, don't drink coffee or alcohol, and even refrain from pot use (one of the major money crops here in British Columbia)... not virtuous, it's just my choice. Vitamin E supplements just might diminish my likelihood of dementia, and vitamins C and E and zinc may slow the progression of macular degeneration, but apart from that I can't find anything that everyone agrees you must take. Apparently a folic acid supplement is recommended by all for the first trimester of pregnancy, but at eighty, that's hardly applicable, although with mothers having children later and later in life, (I just note a seventy-year-old woman in India produced twins through in vitro fertilization) you might like to take a note of this just in case.

- Yes, well, church beliefs and local superstitions and cultural norms might all give support and comfort, but effective treatment can be tested.

- The most important step I can take, apparently, and I use the word "important" advisedly, is to check out the home for loose rugs, things that can be stumbled over, things that can be slipped on. As you age, fractures and breaks from falls are the most life-threatening events. You don't even have to work out the cost-benefits of this move. It's all benefit, and compared with all the above...so simple.

Two more bits for my desk – which is now cluttered with advice:

Unpleasant human feelings and difficult behaviour are not diseases.

Distress is complex.

No, of course I don't have time to do enough research to work out what I need just now in the way of any kind of treatment, I'm busy writing poetry, so I just haven't been near a doctor with anything worse than a blackened toenail since my mastectomy eight years ago. Abstaining from both the allopathic and alternative medicine worlds in this way seems to work very well for me, for oddly enough I feel remarkably healthy for an eighty-year-old.

Again, please remember these are just the siftings of my readings from books on aging and it is on some of these selections that I will base my future behaviour in life. You might read the same books and come to totally different, and just as valid, conclusions. We each choose our own way, or, if we can't because genes and chance cause a swerving, we can, at least, choose how we react to the hand we've been given.

On Reading Poetry at Eighty

I read poetry at seventy-nine
and the world went "Ho Hum,"
as it does for readings
of most poetry.
The next day I'm eighty,
and people are suddenly agog
at my words.
"Imagine," they say,
"Writing that and she's eighty!"
It's amazing what one day counts for.
It's as if I'm a nine-day wonder;
a performing dog, standing
on its hind legs smoking a pipe,
or a three-year-old in cowboy boots
belting out a Patsy Cline number.
I feel the patting of hands
on my head, and wonder to myself
"Whatever will they say when
I'm reading my poetry at ninety?"

On Being Liminal

It was during a brief stay in Morocco in my late thirties that I first became fascinated with doorways. The Moorish doorways there had me entranced. Their shapes presented a positive and negative, as I concentrated first on the brickwork of the outline and then on the space it defined; the space that beckoned me in, and threatened me with the unknown at the same time. I would stand for ages leaning up against doorposts, my feet on the threshold, in some kind of odd daze, indecisive, floating, unwilling to take action. It was a vulnerable time in my life, for it was during this stay in Morocco that I decided to leave my first husband. Liminal comes from the Latin word for threshold, *limen*, and liminal is what I felt then and what I have felt for a large part of my life.

Liminal is a word constantly used in books on aging, but here I'd like to explore it from a more personal angle. Liminal defines an in-between stage of neither this nor that

– still baby but almost child; still child but almost adolescent, still adolescent but needing to be adult; still adult but...ah, there's the rub. Liminal people are on the doorstep, the margin, and while we are all familiar with the stage that the baby, the child and the adolescent will be moving into when they cross the threshold, when it comes to an adult moving through to death, it's unknownness makes the liminality of old age quite another matter. At all other life passages, we may be fearful, we may shake, we may fall to pieces, but we will inevitably settle, maybe awkwardly, maybe hesitantly, but quite definitely into the next stage of life that beckons, for it is not unfamiliar. The uncomfortable marginality while we are in transition is bearable because although we may be rejected by our juniors in age, and not yet be accepted by our seniors, we know that eventually we will adopt a lot of the outward signs of the stage we are moving into. With old age it is another matter. It is as if we are being pushed into the margins by neglect and omission and left there to fend for ourselves best as we can. Unlike the other thresholds in our lives, society offers no ritual of support to us in order to move on, there are no rules guiding us as to how we should grow old, or deal with sickness and death. Marginalization into old-old age pushes us towards the unknown stage of "after death." We are offered no clues for this stage so that we can prepare. Religion offers beliefs, but nothing for sure. Because of our increasing lifespan, this final transition period could last twenty or even thirty years. That is a long time to be uncomfortable.

Earlier in this book I have dealt with the extreme pushes society gives the aged, the pushes of dismissal as society regards our age group as irrelevant; the pushes of neglect that to all intents and purposes amount to geronticide. Here I want to stay with us as liminal beings, ghosts as it were, stuck in limbo. We have been stripped of the social status of being employed and therefore useful. We have become powerless because of declining bodily functions, and, worse still, we are regarded as some kind of threat to the good of the community at large. Threat in that we need the labours of young adults to support our pensions and to pay for our medical expenses. As we grow in number and the birth rate drops, we, the aged, will be making larger demands on fewer people. This may, the economists point out, reach an untenable point. Paradoxically then, the more harmless we become, the bigger threat we are. The most marginalized of us all are aged, immigrant, visible minority women. The least? White, Anglo-Saxon, wealthy males who have attended the right schools and universities. The old school tie that bands them together rules the world at the moment and takes them with least pain into their later years.

The problem, as I see it, is how to live liminally and be positive. How to stay in a state of the unknown, living on the threshold, and yet achieve some comfort in that position and gain some respect, which, of course, starts with self-respect? First, there is strength in numbers. When enough people are pushed to the margin, the margin becomes a valid place to be – the minority becomes a group to be reckoned with. Secondly, we each, individually, can give ourselves validity, even though the ruling group may be dismissive of us. You count as a human being, even if you are confined to a wheelchair or on life support. You must count yourself, if you expect others to count you.

I was born of Jewish parents in a non-Jewish community. I was born a twin. My grandparents were immigrants and my parents still bore traces of the immigrant mindset. Also, our family was of a below-middle class in a very class-conscious society. That gave me four immediate areas to deal with in which I was liminal – immigrant stigma, odd birth stigma, inferior class stigma, and racial-religious stigma. How did I deal with all these? Well until I became conscious of what a fringe person I was, it didn't seem to matter. As soon as I became conscious of my liminality, I became shy, I stammered, I became overactive and a nuisance as I rushed this way and that trying to fit in to too many desirable roles that I was ill-equipped to adopt. How could I rub out my Jewishness, my immigrant grandparents, our family's financial inadequacies, my twinship? It was an impossible task for an adolescent. It wasn't until I was forty that I once again became that small child who rose above all distinctions, only this time I was aware of what I was dealing with. Everyone needs to reach this position, this gaining of one's own voice, for it is the strength of your own core that will help you deal with all the thresholds you have to step over in life – marriage, parenthood, loss, declining body... death. So we are back to the two ways of dealing with the marginalization of the aged – the external one of banding together with similar people, and the internal one of staying grounded in your own being. Once the liminalization is accepted, it, paradoxically, no longer counts.

Twilight, autumn, doorways, the time from dreams to wakening, the times when tides turn are all things I love and embrace. Although liminal, they are not necessarily times and places of sadness and bewilderment, although they can be. They are also times and places of potential, of opportunity, of a certain flexibility which allows us to move in any known, or unknown, direction...a time and a place to embrace.

Things on the Edge

Things on the edge
always seem more
interesting, since,
like Janus, they face
both this way and that.
Trees on the fringe of forests
grow more vigorously;
waves as they crash the shore
link continents far apart;
our skin that interfaces
the flesh within and
the reality without
protects, but keeps us
also imprisoned.
Border people, who stay on
the fringe, can see more clearly
the moments of bittersweet...
the moments when laughter
edges into tears.

Death and Dying Head On

We enter the race when we are born and we leave it when we die. Why learn to drive your chariot better when you are close to the finishing post? All you have to consider then is how to make your exit. If an old man has something to learn, it is the art of dying, and this is precisely what occupies people least at my age; we think of anything rather than that.

– Jean-Jacques Rousseau, *Reveries of the Solitary Walker*

Death from old age is rare in animals and, until recently, in humans too. Currently, we can die of old age, though I was surprised to learn that in most countries it is illegal to die of old age. Apparently something more substantial has to go on the record of death. However, on average, such a death is preceded by ten years of chronic ill health. As Dr. Guy Brown says, "Death is no longer an event, it has become a long, drawn-out process." This is because medicine has changed previous quick deaths into chronic disease, e.g., from full-blown AIDS to a chronic-care sexually transmitted disease, from cancer death to cancer disability, from heart attack to heart failure, from stroke into vascular dementia.

This promised ten years of chronic disease and disability will blend in with all the other woes that aging brings such as loss of function and our marginalization. Machines can keep our kidneys going and our failing lungs functioning; we can be drip-fed should our alimentary system fail; bones and joints can be replaced; pacemakers help our faltering heart and, *in extremis*, our heart can be restarted. Instead of dying fairly quickly from infection, as we did in the past, we can now totter along and enrich the pharmaceutical industry for those extra ten years. We are actually more likely to suffer a long period of pain than the poorest peasant in days gone by. It is people living with chronic diseases that are driving up our health costs. Two thirds of all health care spending goes to people with chronic diseases.

It may sound very cynical, but it seems that curing disease doesn't pay. As Dr. Guy Brown says, "you lose your patient – whereas converting an acute disease into a chronic disease pays very handsomely indeed – because you convert a short-term patient into a long-term consumer of your drugs." To die by infectious disease or heart attack is fast; to die from a chronic disease is to be condemned to a slow death.

To be fair, many of these medical, technical and pharmaceutical innovations are made in the interest of lengthening our lives. But these measures are often taken because death is no longer considered a natural process, not just because it pays the pharmaceutical industry. This attitude increases our fear of death, which, in turn, increases both our own and our doctor's desire to intervene heroically.

The cult of youth and the avoidance of the subject of death are both the result of the population age distortion by the baby boomers and our own growing non-participation in the actual process of death. As death is moved from happening in the home to being a hospital event, we no longer take part in the passage. Unless you are religious, there are no social structures that support your role in death and dying anymore.

A while ago, a friend, who was trying to cope with the nearing death of a relative, came to visit. I asked her how she felt about it, and she replied that often she felt she had come to terms with death and was quite calm about the approaching death of her loved one. Other times she panicked frantically trying to fight off the inevitable. I was relieved to hear all this because my ambivalence was getting troubling. If one has a faith with clear beliefs about the afterlife, then death must be much less of a puzzle or a problem; it would be merely a passing over into a fairly well-defined state of being. For those of us who don't have such reassurances, approaching dying can be a little more difficult.

Rationally one can see that the body dissolves into its elements, but how to deal with the "me," who wants and clings to survival? Intellectually, I understand that the "me" does not really exist since it consists of memories and current experiences of the senses, but emotionally I am rather attached to the illusion of "me." I find, on examining my attitudes carefully, that I actually have moments when I have a vague belief, a belief that I might survive in some form or other. Not as an angel playing on a harp, nor as a condemned person, destined to the tortures of Hell, but as some possibly contributing particle, some small element in the evolution of whatever is evolving. This amazes me as I thought I had moved on beyond clinging to the illusory ego, but apparently not.

It seems that Canada is not the best place in the world to die. Britain is. For there palliative care and hospice accommodation is considered a priority. Canada may be great for supplying medication, but the general policy of making dying as dignified a process as is possible does not seem to be of national importance. According to the Canadian Hospice Palliative Care Association, if you have to die in Canada, better move fast to Victoria, Edmonton or Niagara Falls. Victoria I can understand, for it has always been the city of the newlywed and the nearly dead. Edmonton is a puzzle. Could it have anything to do with its giant mall? Niagara Falls also is not an obvious choice, although water spray from the falls, that is frozen on the trees in winter, is a sight that anyone would welcome to see before dying; it is so fairyland and spectacular.

With good palliative care, the patient is assured minimum pain, remains more mobile, and can possibly live up to three months longer, which may include being able to attend a daughter's wedding, or a grandchild's graduation. Unfortunately some specialists don't quite see it this way. For example, there seems to be a running battle between oncologists who view cancer as an enemy to be battled to the last man (or woman), and palliative care workers who have realistically "given up" and just want the sick person's last few months to be as positive as possible. As Dr. Sherwin Nuland points out, "Rather than seeking ways to help his patient face the reality that life must soon come to an end, [the physician] indulges a very sick person and himself in a form of medical 'doing something' to deny the hovering presence of death." Doing more is likely to help the doctor's need rather than the patient's.

Doctors, because of their own fear of death, or perhaps of litigation, often perform uncalled-for treatment in order to extend life while at the same, paradoxically, they are reluctant to treat older patients, sometimes offering less chemo and radiation, less screening to monitor chronic diseases, less anti-clotting treatments for heart disease and definitely under-treatment for mental health problems. Such holding back is a form of ageism. Dr. Mervyn Singer actually claims that people die in intensive care units because the medics lose interest in the patient or decide to conserve resources, not because the body gives up. It's natural then that doctors express an overwhelming desire that they themselves should die at home! Unfortunately in North American, because litigation has become almost second nature, most acutely ill patients are sent to intensive care. It's such a pity that doctors are not trained to understand the aged and that few medical schools offer adequate classes in geriatric medicine.

When I am frightened of anything in life, I find that if I explore it and examine it in all ways, it loses its sting to a certain extent. I remember when I was afraid of heights, I allowed myself to be persuaded to climb a high, steep hill in Morocco. At the top, I walked out on a ledge of rock and, looking down calmly into the valley below, I shouted out to the women working in the fields below (bright as beetles in their colourful dresses), "I love you." And that was the end of my height phobia.

Death is a little more difficult to approach than the fear of heights, but after reading Dr. Sherwin B. Nuland's brilliant book *How We Die: Reflections on Life's Final Chapter* I felt I had stepped a little closer to familiarity. Supporting my investigation of things I fear, Dr. Nuland says, "it is by knowing the truth and being prepared for it that we rid ourselves of that fear of the terra incognita of death that leads to self-deception and disillusions." His account of the actual bodily changes that we go through in most of the common ways of dying certainly reduces that fear of the unknown. In describing the dying process he covers "the stoppage of circulation, the inadequate transport of oxygen to tissues, the flickering out of brain function, the failure of organs, the destruction of vital centers." As Dr. Nuland describes them, "these are the weapons of every horseman of death."

Still, haven't we already died several times – seven according to Shakespeare (infant, schoolboy, lover, soldier, justice, pantaloon, second childhood) – so surely there is nothing special about an old person dying? I spoke earlier of these passings from one stage to another, complaining that there were no rituals to take us over into what many view as the final stage. However, if we adopt the current views of neurologists and psychologists that we are made up of many components that come into being and pass away, changing by the second, then death might no longer seem so definite and so threatening a stage to move into.

I haven't spoken yet about choosing to die. It is Dr. Brogden, in his book on geronticide, who covers the topic of euthanasia head-on. He finds it dangerous since it may very well not be voluntary, being influenced by pressures from relatives, medical staff and people firmly fixed in the ideology that euthanasia is a societally useful process. He feels the "right to die" could so easily slip over into the "duty to die." Artificially prolonging life, he feels, is not right, but artificially deciding a person should "let go" is also not right. In Holland, Dutch euthanasia practice, Dr. Brogden points out, has given more and more power to doctors. Here, of course, the living will and the power of attorney ease euthanasia-like decisions. Brogden also states that "a long-term process of dying may create burdens for others; but personal decisions for suicide amongst the elderly can also have consequences for others." On the other hand, for there is always another hand, the elderly should not be treated like children who can't make intelligent decisions, and when they say "Enough" they shouldn't have to jump off a bridge, or drown themselves to ask for a simple and dignified way out. Apparently, moral decisions have to be made from the time we learn "do" and "don't" until the moment of death.

But I find moral decisions easier to deal with than the euphemisms we use to avoid saying that a person has died. What is it with euphemisms? I swear that I will cry if I hear "passed on" one more time! Passed on? Passed on to where? There seems to be no agreement as to where the person may have passed on to and, indeed, some beliefs would use the word "returning" rather than "passed on" and even they don't know how the "passed-on" person will return – in what shape or guise.

What a lot of euphemisms we have for death and dying. I decided to collect a few and group them into ones concerning the "dying process" and others describing the "definitely dead."

Dying: to croak, to give up the ghost, kick the bucket, to check out, to breathe their last gasp

Dead: in Abraham's bosom, sleeping the big sleep, gone to one's narrow bed, gone to one's reward, met one's maker, gone to feed the fishes, pushing up the daisies, bite the dust, buy the farm, cashed in one's chips, bit the big one, pegged it, turned their toes up, popped their clogs, fallen off their perch (remember the brilliant dead parrot skit by Monty Python?), gone South, gone West, gone home to California, shuffled off this mortal coil (*Hamlet*), joined the choir invisible, run down the curtain, assumed room temperature, taking a dirt nap, checking out the grass from underneath, six feet under, is worm food, with his Father, upon his shield, paid the ferryman, crashed and burned, hitched a ride with the Reaper, toast, sleeping with the fishes, immortally challenged, kicked the oxygen habit, wearing a cement overcoat, taken by the ghost, permabanned, fell off the twig, sitting at God's right hand, paid the price, back to where he came from, gone to Davy Jones's locker, no longer with us.

The euphemisms that I have listed are distasteful to me, and yet, to be fair, they do seem to encapsulate a lot of folklore, so maybe I'll back down enough to say that there are some colourful, descriptive, even frank ways of alternately saying "he or she is definitely dead," that it would be sad to lose. And yet...dead is dead.

At one time my husband and I thought we might be good at Theatresports so we went to a workshop. We weren't good enough...not fast enough, not imaginative enough, with minds not dirty enough. Failure. One exercise stayed with me though. The participants lined up and had to run on stage and kill themselves. The only rule was that the individual mustn't repeat a chosen method. I remember one riotous attempt where the person had acquired a toy car from somewhere and ran themselves over repeatedly with it. Not funny? Actually it was very funny. How serious we are about death, and how obliquely we face it, don't we?

prepared at birth…
now the time has come
there's just confusion

this world's a mess
it's time to go and yet…
spring blossom

the hill is frosted.
my heart wants to travel but
my feet say "Not yet"

when I die and go
to Buddha's Seventh Heaven,
he'll serve me sashimi

reading the obituaries
I absent-mindedly stroke
my liver-spotted hands

When I'm Old and Frail

I should perhaps start by describing the state I might eventually be in when I make the requests I'll be making below. Fragile is a way people define themselves (if they still can) when they can no longer use the traditional medical system of office visits and hospital tests, unless they go by ambulance. They usually have multiple illnesses and it's a toss-up as to which one will take them over. They are dependent on others for their daily needs and they need comfort before medication – unless the medication relieves pain. They are not a homogeneous group and need to be treated as individuals. Standard guidelines are not for them. With the understanding that I may at some time reach this state, I am making the following requests of the universe:

- That my husband, Eli, be with me to the end (in our little vinyl-sided, mortgage-free cottage, if possible). He's a good listener.
- That I have a doctor attending, who, like Dr. John Sloan, makes house calls, treats each person individually and aims for comfort. I would like that they discuss my

diagnosis and prognosis with me and discuss all that is involved in the dying process. I would like to be able to give some input into how my last days will be handled. I would also like them to respect me when I say "Enough's enough." Regarding Dr. Sloan, I recall Kapuściński's comment, "There is so much crap in this world, and then suddenly, there is honesty and humanity." That's Dr. Sloan.

- I do not want heroic measures taken when I have a crisis, nor endless tests that are futile – no bone density tests for my osteoporosis, no measuring of my blood pressure or my cholesterol level. I will be on my way out and don't want tests wasted on me that might profit a younger person. Not fighting a terminal illness is just as brave as fighting one; maybe braver.
- I want a few friends to visit occasionally and talk endlessly of books and the writing life, and that our conversations be as truthful as possible.
- I would like to have the opportunity to thank everyone who has sustained and nourished my life.
- That if I need to make amends to anyone, I have the time to do it.
- I don't want to be a burden.
- I can work out, or not be able to work out, the meaning of life for myself, as well as my possible options after death. I do not need more 'spiritual' input.
- I do not want people to pray for me, nor sit plucking mournful guitar tunes while chanting in a language I don't recognize.
- I want a fun wake with bowls of pickled herring and plates of smoked salmon, and for dessert, a cake such as I haven't eaten in years – loaded with calories.

Legacy and Last Words

I, for one, do not care which of these diseases carries me off as long as the leaving is gentle and the legacy meaningful.

– Dr. Nortin Hadler, *Worried Sick*

What will I leave behind? You can't take it with you is a cliché, but nevertheless true. I used to have a cartoon on my desk with that caption. The picture showed a man sitting on a cloud. Below him, from the window of the living room of what was once his house, a piano is leaving, moving skyward, while his widow is trying earnestly to tug it back. I suppose this was my daily reminder to spread my talents about while I was still around.

I've always felt that if you leave an unfilled gap when you die, you've somehow not fulfilled your promise. If there is too big a mourning, you haven't delegated your powers sufficiently in your life. It's a strange idea, but I'll give you an example. When I was working as a therapist, I led a number of groups. When I decided to try other things in my life, the clinic had a dinner party for me and during the dinner the remaining therapists spent most of the time, not singing my praises as I'd hoped, but deciding who would take over which of my groups. By the end of the meal I was all divided up. I wasn't horrified, or even upset, even though I had within that couple of hours become a ghost figure at the clinic. I felt I had left well-qualified people in my place and within a few weeks, even my most devoted clients would have switched loyalties to the new therapists.

As regards legacy in the material sense, my worldly wealth is not enough to keep my adult children hanging around my doorstep pre-dividing my goods. When they call, it is for other reasons. I have left everything to my husband and he, in turn, in his extraordinarily meticulous way, has divided what little we have between our offspring. The resulting diagram, which is in his will, outshines, in complications, a major corporation's balance sheet.

I just heard of someone who, having been given a month to live, went down to her house in Mexico and called in all her neighbours. She then let them choose anything they wanted to take into their homes. What a lovely gesture.

We do worry about who will remember us and how, don't we though? Edith Bunker, in the old sitcom, used to say about her husband, "Archie doesn't know how to worry without getting upset." We should also try not to get too upset, remembering that all passes, even us. Still we would like to leave a legacy even though it may not be a material one.

My twin sister actually bought herself a bench, inscribed with a brass plate, and had it put in the church gardens below her apartment. My nieces were indignant, saying that it should have been their job to donate the bench after she had died. But Ruth, impatient as myself, and also, as myself, perhaps feeling other people wouldn't do as good a job, was satisfied in that she would be leaving a tasteful legacy. She even commissioned an artist to paint a Christmas card showing her sitting on the bench. I thought it looked rather mournful.

Ruth, who seems to have more time to waste than I do, recently suggested I might amuse myself by listing things I would like to take with me in my coffin, as if I was royalty from the past and could surround myself with jewels and servants to serve me in the netherworld. I resisted listing taking my husband with me for I know there is a long line of island women with their eyes on him. The moment I breathe my last, I am certain they will be over with their baked goods. Eli may, indeed, himself have his eye on one or two of them already, although he hasn't made this obvious in any way, to me at least.

So instead, I turn to the I-can-never-read-you-enough books that are on a special shelf to be my companions in the hereafter: *The Remains of the Day* by Kazuo Ishiguro; *The Uses and Abuses of History* by Margaret MacMillan; *84, Charing Cross Road* by Helene Hanff; *Ethel and Ernest* by Raymond Briggs; Montaigne's *Essays*; and Billy Collins' and Wisława Szymborska's poetry. There are also a couple of scarves that I've knitted that feel really comfortable around my neck, that might well warm what will be left of me in the grave.

Our legacy can be in the flesh, by having children – or you could consider cloning which would give you yourself as a complete kind of legacy. It can also be in creativity, writing books, sculpting sculptures, or painting pictures, or in making breakthroughs in science or some other area of knowledge (these are called memes – cultural genes as it were). Perhaps some kind of essence of ourselves might even hang around for a while after we die – some religious beliefs think this happens and that would also be a sort of legacy, in its own way.

While artists and writers can be remembered by their works, revelations of their lives often overwhelm this. So Koestler, a brilliant political commentator who lived through tumultuous years, may only be remembered as a misogynist; Philip Larkin, one of the most popular British poets of the late twentieth century, as a collector of pornography; and Dylan Thomas as a drunkard and a womanizer. Can't we writers ever have our lives separated from our works, in order that the finest of our works reflect us as a legacy with at least some small amount of glory?

Wanting to leave a legacy may also motivate our behaviour at the end of our life. Judge Posner feels "one's deportment in the face of death is an important part of most people's posthumous reputation; their brave words, their stoical demeanor, may be long remembered." In his usual clear-headed, some might unkindly say cynical, way, the judge considers the cost-benefit ratio of this behaviour and feels that in a sense it is selfish. Socrates' manner of death, his mindful watchfulness as his body reacted to a hemlock draught, has always struck me as an amazing act of full-human behaviour, and a lasting legacy, never mind the cost-benefits.

When I was a therapist I used to finish my therapy period by asking my clients to list the good things that their parents had taught them. This was often after weeks of denigration of the monstrous parents, who, when I met them, usually seemed perfectly innocuous and ordinary. Everyone we meet has something useful to offer us and that something is what we can incorporate, so that when the person dies, their influence carries on within us. Irvin Yalom calls this surviving of wisdoms and skills "rippling," and claims it to be a form of legacy. He says "attempts to preserve personal identity are always futile. Transiency is forever. Rippling, as I use it, refers instead to leaving behind something from your life experience; some trait; some piece of wisdom, guidance, virtue, comfort that passes on to others, known, or unknown." What a great idea and so much less demanding than striving for fame and fortune as a way to have one's name carried on. Yalom adds that "the idea of rippling, of passing along to others what has mattered to one life, implies connection with other self-aware essences; without that, rippling is impossible." So staying open and being with others who are also brave enough to stay open means your essence will carry on even if you are not Elvis, or Einstein.

Of course ripplings are often exposed at the time of a person's wake. People pay homage to how they have been touched by the dead one in so many ways. I have been amazed, at the few wakes I've been to, how many people only speak well of the dead.

> at the wake
> I listen to the praise
> and wonder
> if we speak well of everyone
> what value is the "well" we speak of?

I like Nancy K. Miller's rather wise comment on tears at wakes, "Sometimes we can't separate relief from sorrow, resentment from love."

At a wake I went to some years ago, I knew the dead person quite well and so was interested, and surprised, when only two of her four children spoke. When they did, they used the words "parenting difficulties" and "not always seeing eye to eye" which I found refreshingly honest and disarming. I had only known the dead person as an overly generous and kind being and so was amazed at this other side being revealed. I also enjoyed the self-praise, with almost no mention of the deceased, of two handsome, distinguished-looking gentlemen in their late seventies. One was the deceased's first husband, who had taken her on her first trip abroad, and the other, her last lover, who had taken her on her last. They rather delighted in the novelty of their positions and sat happily side-by-side sharing their distinction. Yes, ripplings can be a mixed bag.

Passing on ripplings reminds me of a book I have recently read. It is Randy Pausch's *The Last Lecture*, a series of mini-essays worked around the actual last lecture this computer scientist gave at Mellon University before he died of pancreatic cancer. I didn't want to like the book – I don't, on the whole, go for bestsellers; thought the subject would be depressing; and disliked the sound of his all-American, Disney World family. Which just goes to show how wrong I can be sometimes, for the book, and the lecture, were not about the fact he was dying, but about how he had fulfilled his childhood dreams and how we could do likewise. In the book, he asks the question, "What makes me unique?" That is a question all of us may have asked ourselves sometime in our lives and one worth pondering as we age.

From time to time I worry what my last words will be – never mind my last lecture. I am a voluble talker and would hate my last breath to stop in mid-sentence, or while in the midst of a cliché that I am using because I'm feeling too lazy to phrase my thoughts in more succinct words. Or it would be too bad if my last words caught me being mean-spirited as my twin sometimes accuses me of being.

Japan is a culture where the last words, particularly of well-known poets, esteemed samurai or noted priests, were much prized. Whether poet or samurai, these last words were expected to take the form of a poem. These poems were valued so much that many of these folks would prepare them years ahead (for who knows when the moment of one's death will be) in the form of a tanka, or a haiku, so as not to be caught with less than worthy thoughts during their last moments. Certainly if someone recovered after thinking they would die, there would be the reassuring thought that they now had time to rewrite their last poem.

Being of an obsessive nature, at one time I had thought of collecting these Japanese death poems. They are called *jisei*. In case you might want to prepare your own last verse in readiness now, here are a few of my favourites for you to be inspired by.

A rather up-to-date poem by Utsu, considering it was written in 1863:

> the owner of the cherry blossom
> turns to compost
> for the trees

Here's one by Toko on the sharp reality that indicates a poem won't soften the fact of departure:

> Death poems
> are mere delusion –
> death is death

There are many death poems about fallen petals and empty cicada shells, such as Tanehiko's:

> Such is the world's way:
> in fall the willow
> sheds its leaves

I, of course, prefer the chirpier ones such as Raizan's:

> Raizan has died
> to pay for the mistake
> of being born:
> for this he blames no one,
> and bears no grudge

As a one-time traveller myself, I rather go for the journeying metaphor in Michikaze's

> Today I put on summer
> clothes and journey
> to a world I haven't seen yet

And here's one by Sofu pointing out that none of us know the time of our dying:

> Festival of souls:
> yesterday I hosted them,
> today I am a guest...

And I'll finish with my all-time favourite by Kozan Ichikyo

> Empty-handed I entered the world
> barefoot I leave it.
> my coming, my going –
> two simple happenings
> that got entangled.

Bankei, perhaps understanding life a little deeper than others, proclaimed, "I've lived for seventy-two years. I've been teaching people for forty-five. What I've been telling you and others every day during that time is all my death verse. I'm not going to make another one now, before I die, just because everyone else does it."

Still, I would be happy to die after writing any of the poems above. All these poems have been translated by Yoel Hoffman in his authoritative book on the subject, *Japanese Death Poems: Written by Zen Monks and Haiku Poets on the Verge of Death*. "Kismet, Hardy," Nelson's supposed last words, hardly comes near in interest by comparison.

For myself, I am a bit hesitant to take this last chance to boost my station as a poet and personal essayist. Though given to showing off from time to time, I hesitate to push my ranking by a few clever last lines. Still, now turned eighty, I must confess I have tried a few "last" verses:

> *bird, or bird shit*
> *the haijin seizes her pen*
> *and writes a haiku*

This effort tries to indicate that in my writing, I didn't discriminate when it came to topics about which to write. Some delicate haiku writers tremble at the word "shit."

However the euphemism "poop" just doesn't do the work I want the word to do.

> *will seagulls*
> *lift my unwritten poems*
> *from my grave*
> *and smash them on my tombstone*
> *until they break open?*

or

> *it is inevitable*
> *no matter our five minutes*
> *in the limelight*
> *dust will return to dust...*
> *there's comfort in recycling*

or

> *the last act?*
> *I thought this was*
> *the dress rehearsal*

or

> *hanging up the new calendar*
> *however many years, is it*
> *ever enough?*

None of these quite come near Narihira's wonderful one, which I quoted earlier, but is well worth repeating:

> I have always known
> that at last I would
> take this road, but yesterday
> I did not know that it would be today

Karl Marx, when asked by his housekeeper for last words, said, "Go on, get out – last words are for fools who haven't said enough." Have I said enough, I wonder?

Legacy

What shall I leave – a quilt, a verse
a knitted scarf, an adage – terse?
No, like a cat, I'll leave my smile,
and folks will wonder, love or guile?

these days,
I write in a frenzy
hoping
that my words will leave a mark
on the world, a footstep in the concrete

Looking Death in the Eye

Life is pleasant, death is peaceful. It's the transition that's troublesome.

— Isaac Asimov

When are we actually dead? It is still a matter of controversy. Death seems to be defined currently by a permanent loss of consciousness. As Dr. Guy Brown says, "there is no point worrying about death, because when dead we won't be aware of it." But when are we dead? When we can no longer interact with anybody? When both our body and brain are dead? When our respiration and circulation systems fail?

These days, it is possible to inject neural stem cells into the brain and watch them migrate to damaged areas. Dr. Guy Brown asks, "Supposing they could do this, heal the damaged brain and wake people who have been in a coma? Or supposing a chip inserted in the brain could act similarly. What then?" Our fast-developing medical technology could well demand a redefinition of "death." If bits of us can be repaired, then maybe death isn't so firmly an "alive" or "dead" judgement.

James Hughes, when discussing the future of the idea of ourselves as individuals, suggests that because of the possibility of "identity cloning, distributing one's identity over multiple platforms, sharing of mental components with others, and the merging of several individuals into one identity," there won't be clear-cut lines between individuals anymore. Our present views of ourselves as distinct individuals will move to the idea of ourselves as a conglomeration of processes. As Robert Ettinger declares, "The simplest conclusion is that there is really no such thing as individuality in any profound sense... Let us then cut the Gordian knot by recognizing that identity, like morality, is man-made and relative, rather than natural and absolute." In the future we may not be judged as either alive or dead, there may be all kinds of blends in between. A person may very well be, as Buddhism declares, a process of continual change with no fixed "self" underlying it. However, the future is not here yet and so we still have to come to terms with death as we know it.

Two books that look at death very directly, or rather concern themselves with the anxiety of knowing that death is our fate, are Ernest Becker's brilliant classic about various psychological schools' approach to death anxiety, *The Denial of Death*, and Irvin Yalom's sensitively written *Staring at the Sun: Overcoming the Terror of Death*. These books alone will have you considering, and reconsidering, your feelings about death. They may even persuade you to nudge your basic philosophy of life a little.

Sam Keen, in his foreword to *The Denial of Death*, sums up Becker's approach succinctly, and I précis it here. The world is terrifying and the basic motivation of humans is our need to control our basic anxiety. Thus there is a need to deny the terror of death and so we keep this terror at an unconscious level. Our need to deny our mortality and achieve a heroic self-image is the root of humanly caused evil. Our efforts to be assured we are heroic are damaging, leading often to wars and we need to find a moral way to be heroic that is equivalent. Becker suggests actions such as fighting disease, poverty and oppression. Keen hopes individuals might consider tossing out tribalism and nationalism and searching for a universal ethic.

This is not just a classic, but a powerful book, and I would, therefore, like to quote a little more from it. "[Man] doesn't know who he is, why he was born, what he is doing on the planet, what he is supposed to do, what he can expect." Therefore, full humanness, for Becker, "means full fear and trembling, at least some of the waking day." Becker points out that we protect ourselves by routines, and appear self-confident with our careers and possessions, but are actually "inauthentic" people. He feels that to see the world as it really is "places a trembling animal at the mercy of the entire cosmos and the problem of the meaning of it." I too feel, at eighty, moments of supreme confidence alternating with moments of terror at the fragility of my satisfactory life. Even if (as I do) we channel our fear into creativity, Becker feels the surge of creativity only throws us back to our own insignificance in the universe. Man's paradox, as Becker says so well, is that "he feels agonizingly unique and yet he knows that this doesn't make any difference as far as ultimates are concerned. He has to go the way of the grasshopper; even though it takes longer."

All this may seem a little remote from leg cramps and our disappearing pensions, but actually it is the basis of it all. Self-preservation depends on our fear of death. Somehow the instinct to stay alive is in us from the start.

Knowing one is anxious about death is not the same as experiencing that full anxiety. I have known more realistically since my episode with cancer that I am going to die, yet I had an experience not long ago that made it much more real. It was nothing big and dramatic. Actually it was a very quiet moment when suddenly it was as if every cell of my body knew its mortality. I can't describe it any better than that for it was a deep, yet undramatic moment when death became an inch closer to my understanding of it.

Becker's solutions for this untenable problem of the meaning of life, and, by extension, the meaning of death is that "the only secure truth men have is that which they themselves create and dramatize; to live is to play at the meaning of life.... It teaches us once and for all that childlike foolishness is the calling of mature men." I trust he means women here too and I feel happily in agreement.

Irvin Yalom's book *Staring at the Sun* also presents our anxiety of death as the main motivator of our actions. Yalom's and Becker's books present me with perhaps the most important things I should consider in life – not just my anxiety about death, which has run my whole life apparently, but more importantly the question of whether I have lived an "unlived life." I reckon that the more "lived" our life has been, the lower our death anxiety. Folks with such anxiety often accumulate wealth, seek power, may be excessively religious...all of which are tactics that they hope will bring them some kind of immortality.

For Dr. Yalom the possible state of non-being after death is not terrifying for, as he points out, he won't know he is not existing. But can those of us with little or no concept of the afterlife be so philosophical about this? The notion of the ephemerality of all things only sharpens our life, he feels. *"The way to value life, the way to feel compassion for others, the way to love anything with greatest depth is to be aware that these experiences are destined to be lost"* (italics original).

And speaking of possible scenarios for our afterlife, I just loved the book *Sum: Forty Tales from the Afterlives* by neuro-scientist David Eagleman, in which he imagines a startling number of afterlife conditions that appear amusing and yet each is latched on to a deep bit of philosophy. Take the wonderful scenario of the afterlife where we relive our life, but in blocks of activities, e.g., we spend six weeks waiting for a green light, fifty-one days deciding what to wear, etc. This is witty and probably fairly accurate – except I would spend at least six months doing the laundry, rather than the three he suggests – but it also makes us ponder how much of our time we do spend on idle things. Other afterlives he presents include one in which there are only people you remember – so there are no strangers around, and an afterlife where you can choose to relive your life but with one change. The change suggested is that you choose immortality and we all know what happens to that kind of Faustian choice. My favourite afterlife is called "Quantum" and here you live all possibilities at once, including mutually exclusive ones. This, of course, proves exhausting for you, and so the angel narrows it down to you being in a closed room, one-on-

one with your lover. The result is hilarious and so close to home!

I have no notion of what my afterlife might be, but I did have an odd experience during my first cancer lumpectomy at age forty that gave me pause for thought. It was at a difficult time in my life and I had admitted myself to hospital on my own. The night before surgery I imagined I would be waking with one breast missing. I thought of all the things in my life that would drop away – lovers, a body image where I am whole, certain paths in life. Suddenly I seemed to slip into a void where "I," that is "me," had disappeared and yet, and yet there was something remaining. It was hard to put into words then and harder now, but from time to time I wonder what that experience was all about and whether it might not be similar to that of after-death.

Proving the soul, or anything else come to that, does or doesn't exist appears to be very difficult from a philosophical standpoint. If it makes you happy, what's the harm though? Unicorns, angels, Father Christmas, souls... Maybe we folk, who demand proof all the while, are not as content with life as those with beliefs for which there is no evidence. None of us have a truly accurate idea of "reality." Our senses allow us a very small window onto it, but how about the universe beyond the senses and beyond our present technical ability to extend them?

Multiple universes, life on other planets, our own life happening here and elsewhere at the same time...these ideas are science fiction at the moment, but suppose they are more than possibilities. What then? What if the "soul" is some kind of immortal principle that we hold? Maybe our memes and our genes are our soul or, as Dr. Guy Brown suggests, maybe the soul is consciousness. If we are permanently changing beings doesn't that kind of remove death's sting and count as us having a kind of immortality already? Oh dear, I do ask the strangest questions.

Many doctors seem unwilling to discuss death with their patients. This is unfair as most of us have "unfinished business" and knowing we have a limited time to deal with it is important. Yet knowing is not a simple act. For example, not long ago a friend of mine was close to death. When I visited, he told me of a peculiar insight he had had recently. A hospice worker had been visiting to offer help, because dying presents complicated procedures not only for the person dying, but also for the survivors – things such as how to dispose of the body and deal with the will. My friend was listening politely when suddenly he was struck with the insight that it was he who was dying. Of course he knew that, but he hadn't really allowed himself to know completely. After he had told me this I decided not to visit him again, because it is this insight that we all need, and having had it, I felt he required all his remaining energy to die the way he would prefer to and did not need a load of visitors to distract him.

A wonderful literary example of no one wanting to discuss death with a patient is Tolstoy's brilliant novella *The Death of Ivan Ilych*. Of it Vera Klement comments, "The people around him, family, doctors, are evasive; they lie to him or avoid him because they don't know how to speak, how to acknowledge that he is dying. It is to him an experience of utter humiliation and abandonment. In the process of dying he becomes socially unacceptable. An outcast. His death is seen, in the end, as an irritating interruption of a card game."

Read it. It is a devastating example of not being able to speak of death and dying clearly.

It seems to me that dying with dignity must be an incredibly difficult thing to do. As Philip Roth points out, "trying to die isn't like trying to commit suicide – it may actually be harder, because what you are trying to do is what you least want to have happen; you dread it, but there it is, and it must be done, and by no one but you."

Have I Learned Anything?

Are we, the elderly, victims of oppression, or spoilt, pampered parasites? Is it an "us" versus "them" situation with younger generations? We naturally don't always understand groups to which we don't belong but are we guilty of prejudice ourselves? What are the reasons we older folk are not respected as maybe we once were? Is it that our wisdom and experience no longer matter in a fast-changing world? Will the young be persuaded that the high cost of caring for the aged is worthwhile? All these questions I have considered to some extent in this book, and I am still pondering them.

The conclusions I have come to are personal ones of course. I have not been given the talent for initiating widespread reforms or even of introducing possible solutions, but here are some recommendations to myself that others might like to consider:

I should make the last ten years of my life worth living because apparently they are going to be tough. But, as I don't know when those last ten years will start, I'd better begin right now. I should stop pretending I'm not going to die and start preparing for it in necessary ways – possible organ donation, making a living will, funeral preparations, disposition of my material possessions, etc. I could take a look at the "natural death" movement, a kind of do-it-yourself death at home without too many professionals involved and a disposal of the body in an environmentally sensible kind of way (not taking up good agricultural land, for example). I'd better get writing and get those books out for that's my real legacy, I feel. If there is funding for dementia research I should contribute. If there are protests about drug companies working for medicines for chronic illnesses instead of channelling the money into cures, I'll protest that too.

Generally, if I can get through the day with my integrity even vaguely intact, if I can maintain some kind of a faith in the goodness of humanity, awe at the complexity of the universe and joy that I am still part of the whole process, then that is a day well-spent, I think.

My own life journey has taken me to some strange places – a lunatic asylum in the Caribbean, the inmates in chains; a temple in the Himalayas where human skull cups were full of strange liquids and the thigh-bone trumpet blew a sound dredged up from the depths; sleeping on a grass mat in Morocco and being woken by a wild boar rushing past; dragging myself under a hedge in New Zealand, sick from goodness knows what and feeling that it was a great place to die, should I die at that moment – the list of my exotic experiences seems endless. What I was searching for in my travels I haven't the slightest idea, only that the search was urgent and took me away from family and friends and a steady income and any kind of security. I wore exotic clothes, and shabby clothes, and nylons with straight seams and lace gloves, Zen robes, kimono and full Islamic burka. None of this helped, although I must have thought it might at the time. It was all part of coming home to a home I didn't know I had, I guess. And so I wandered this way and that until I did the simple thing of accepting where I was at that moment. After this decision, anywhere and any moment was a good enough home for me.

I'd like to finish this chapter with a poem about my pilgrimage for maybe it can help you with yours.

Pilgrimage

I've been to the Himalayas
searching with one hundred thousand
full-length prostrations for roads
that led to Lhasa;
I've wandered the hills of the Lake District
seeking the magic words of distant poets
in the hopes that they would inspire
a few of my own;
I've sailed the oceans to find
even more distant seers,
myself in Zen robes, or covered
in the ribbons of secret initiations
or the beaded headdress of temptresses,
muttering a thousand mantra.

Yesterday, I paused at the step
of our small vinyl-sided cottage,
myself in gumboots and shabby
garden clothes.
The smells from the kitchen cheered my spirit
and glimpses of the well-worn recycled furniture
appeased my Puritan instinct and

the pieces of our creative name reminded me
of the energies needed to bring the golem to life...
and suddenly, aware of the wealth within,
I took my simple pilgrimage over the threshold.

Hank's Wake

The number of funerals I have attended in my life could be counted on one hand. The number of wakes perhaps stretches onto the second hand. For me, living on an island means that I am living more intimately with a community than at any other time in my life. I know hundreds of people on Gabriola, and would recognize maybe closer to five hundred. They have eaten at our kitchen table, attended my book launches and Eli's sculpture shows, and we have also supported them in their own academic or creative endeavours. We contribute to the food bank, that even on our small island we unfortunately need, and pay a little each month towards the mortgage at The Commons, a property the island owns in common (the first such phenomena in Canada, apparently) and which serves the community in good times and bad. All this to say I am more inclined to participate in the various gatherings that go on on Gabriola Island than I have been willing to in places I have lived at other times in my life, since the folk here are part of my life and a substitute for my far-flung family.

Having a supportive community, not to mention a supportive partner, makes not only for a longer life, but for a sweeter one. Hank and Alison had been our close friends for years. We had shared ups and downs, as friends do, and given each other loads of advice that we rarely acted on. Hank was a complex, clever, but ornery guy. He had strong opinions and strong ideas and could rarely be sidetracked from them. If a path was to be chosen, he selected the most complicated one and the one least likely to lead to success. And yet, in the years we knew him, he built both a cottage and a hefty house on their seven acres. He was short in stature, and it always amazed me that those colossal timbers used in the main house had somehow been hauled into place by him, and that they still stood firm.

A year before he died, he was diagnosed with pancreatic cancer and went through the usual attempts at restraining it as best he could. When he finally returned to Gabriola, we all knew that it was to spend his last months with his wife, Alison, and his community with as much joy, and as little pain, as possible.

His last moments alone with his wife reminded me so much of Kay Redfield Jamison's beautifully expressed last moments with her husband: "The intimacy in being together during the approach of death is unimaginable. We knew that what he was going through was final. We lay so close to each other in our bed that we were aware of everything that went on in the other's body. It was a long and private farewell." And as poet Douglas Dunn said about the last days with his wife, "Sad? Yes. But it was beautiful also. / There was a stillness in the world. Time was out."

Hank's wake was wonderfully jubilant...well, jubilant and sad also for the memories were a mixture of telling of the funny events in his life, and also expressions of sadness at his death. As I said before, it often worries me that at wakes people only say good of the dead. They never show the full picture of a rich human being; a person full of the virtues and the sins that make us human.

When it came to my turn to offer some words, I chose to fill out Hank's image a little. I said, "Hank was an ornery man, but not an ordinary one. He was stubborn and obstinate, but was the hardest on himself for, if something had to be done, Hank always chose the most convoluted and complicated path. When asked about his decisions he always seemed to have good reasons for making them, although those too were complicated and convoluted. Yet, when friends, or his community, had needs, Hank was straightforward and spontaneous in his generosity and often anonymous."

I then read a couple of tanka I had written for the occasion. One was specifically for Hank:

> *has he gone then*
> *to some building site*
> *in the beyond*
> *still stockpiling planks*
> *that might be useful one day?*

Having given much thought to the occasion, since a close friend's death inevitably draws you to think of your own, I also offered a tanka for everyone present, a wondering of where Hank might be, supposing that any part of us survives the dying process:

is that
all life is then…
a constant journey
where even after death
one hasn't arrived?

At one point during the event, a group got up and danced and sang "Mayim, Mayim," as joyful a celebratory dance as one would ever wish to perform. It was written in the thirties to celebrate the finding of water in the Israeli desert and "Water, Water" is how the title translates. Water is a big concern on our island as we rely on wells and cisterns. It was also a big concern to Hank, both as a participating member of our community and personally as his concrete cisterns leaked from time to time, as concrete cisterns often do, leaving him and Alison without water for drinking and washing. So yes, "Mayim, Mayim" was such an appropriate dance at Hank's wake.

When the spoken offerings had drawn to a close, the MC announced that Hank had requested cake and ice cream be served, and so a gigantic cake came forth and we all indulged in the sweetness of it, remembering the sweetness of Hank's generous nature and of all the work he had put in to help our island stay as close to its natural state as possible.

The day after the wake, Alison came over to our place and we spoke gently of the life they had lived together. I noticed she had on one of Hank's old sweaters. He had worn it up to the end as it was soft and comforting. I found it very touching and wrote:

the day
after he died
she started
to wear his old sweater
the bottom edge unravelling

A Reader's Bibliography

Becker, Ernest, *The Denial of Death*

Blackman, Sushila, *Graceful Exits: How Great Beings Die*

Bortz, Walter M., and Randall Stickrod, *The Roadmap to 100: The Breakthrough Science of Living a Long and Healthy Life*

Brogden, Mike, *Geronticide: Killing the Elderly*

Brown, Guy, *The Living End: The Future of Death, Aging and Immortality*

Darling, David, *Zen Physics: The Science of Death, the Logic of Reincarnation*

De Grey, Aubrey, with Michael Rae, *Ending Aging: The Rejuvenation Breakthroughs That Could Reverse Human Aging in Our Lifetime*

Dychtwald, Ken, *Age Power: How the 21st Century Will Be Ruled by the New Old*

Eagleman, David, *Sum: Forty Tales from the Afterlives*

Fishman, Ted C., *Shock of Gray: The Aging of the World's Population and How it Pits Young Against Old, Child Against Parent, Worker Against Boss, Company Against Rival, and Nation Against Nation*

Friedan, Betty, *The Fountain of Age*

Green, Lyndsay, *You Could Live a Long Time: Are You Ready?*

Hadler, Nortin M., *Worried Sick: A Prescription for Health in an Overtreated America*

Hoffmann, Yoel, ed., *Japanese Death Poems: Written by Zen Monks and Haiku Poets on the Verge of Death*

Hollander, Nicole, *Tales of Graceful Aging from the Planet Denial*

Jacoby, Susan, *Never Say Die: The Myth and Marketing of the New Old Age*

Jamison, Kay Redfield, *Nothing was the Same*

Jerome, John, *On Turning Sixty-Five: Notes from the Field*

Manguel, Alberto, *Stevenson Under the Palm Trees*

Moynihan, Ray, and Alan Cassels, *Selling Sickness: How the World's Biggest Pharmaceutical Companies are Turning Us All into Patients*

Nuland, Sherwin B., *How We Die: Reflections on Life's Final Chapter*

Posner, Richard A., *Aging and Old Age*

Dass, Ram, *Still Here: Embracing Aging, Changing, and Dying*

Rosofsky, Ira, *Nasty Brutish and Long: Adventures in Old Age and the World of Eldercare*

Roszak, Theodore, *The Making of an Elder Culture: Reflections on the Future of America's Most Audacious Generation*

Rubin, Lillian B., *60 on Up: The Truth About Aging in America*

Schachter-Shalomi, Zalman, and Ronald S. Miller, *From Age-ing to Sage-ing: A Profound New Vision of Growing Older*

Schwalbe, Robert, *Sixty, Sexy, and Successful: A Guide for Aging Male Baby Boomers*

Scott-Maxwell, Florida, *The Measure of My Days: One Woman's Vivid, Enduring Celebration of Life and Aging*

Sloan, John, *A Bitter Pill: How the Medical System is Failing the Elderly*

Tolstoy, Leo, *The Death of Ivan Ilych*

Wakan, Naomi Beth, *Late Bloomer: On Writing Later in Life*

Welch, H. Gilbert, *Overdiagnosed: Making People Sick in the Pursuit of Health*

Willetts, David, *The Pinch: How the Baby Boomers Took Their Children's Future – And Why They Should Give it Back*

Yalom, Irvin D., *Staring at the Sun: Overcoming the Terror of Death*

Zimmerman, Lillian, *Bag Lady or Powerhouse?: A Roadmap for Midlife (Boomer) Women*

Resources

When looking for original solutions for keeping the aged within their own homes and for a community who is interested in novel solutions for meeting the needs of their aged, I found these sites had very inventive ideas. I am not overly familiar with any of these sites and am definitely not endorsing any products they might have to sell, but if you would like to improve the condition of the aged in your community, please check them out, for they are full of fresh and economical solutions.

Firstly for an excellent overview:

Intel's Global Aging Experience Study
http://www.intel.com/Assets/PDF/Article/Aging_From_People_to_Prototypes_and_Products_article.pdf

Intel and General Electric have focused on helping isolated older people. In their own words:

Senior citizens are increasingly lonely, and it's a serious problem. According to a study by the Public Library of Science Medicine–loneliness as a health risk factor is twice as detrimental as being obese, and equal to the risk of smoking cigarettes and alcoholism.

That's why Intel-GE Care Innovations recently launched Care Innovations Connect, an easy-to-use, tablet-based digital platform that aims to combat social isolation among seniors. Care Innovations is a company formed from a combination of GE Healthcare's Home Health Division and Intel's Digital Health Group.

The Connect software acts as both an in-home digital device for seniors, and a customized portal that can be used by professional caregivers. The platform includes wellness surveys, wellness data, a community calendar and other tools – like a webcam and social network – making it sort of like a Facebook for seniors, in tablet form.

http://www.gereports.com/facebook-for-seniors-battling-social-isolation-and-loneliness-among-the-elderly-with-a-tablet/

Other initiatives:

Aconchego, Portugal
http://www.bonjoia.org

A clever program in which seniors invite university students to live in their homes, and as a result the students help to decrease the seniors' feelings of loneliness and isolation, promoting the welfare of seniors and their families.

Canadian Association of Retired Persons (CARP), Canada
http://www.carp.ca/

CARP is a national, non-profit organization based in Toronto and has information on health, money, family, leisure, home, learning, travel, chat rooms and discussion forums.

Canadian Senior Years, Canada
http://www.senioryears.com

In their own words, "Here you will find the best information, articles, news and Canadian site links available for seniors on the web today! In addition, we provide a place for seniors to gather and trade information through our email pals and single seniors listings, senior talent page and articles."

Elder Power, United States
http://www.lincme.net/

An organization that provides, for a monthly fee, almost all of the services a nursing home could at a fraction of the cost. Home visits, phone calls, camera and motion-sensor monitoring, transportation, help with meals and bathing can be included in the monthly fee. This allows the elderly to stay in their own homes, though incapacitated.

Experience Corps, United States
http://www.experiencecorps.org

Experience Corps is a program which engages people over fifty-five as tutors for elementary school students, to help teachers in the classroom, and to lead after-school enrichment activities. As they say on their website, "independent research shows that Experience Corps boosts student academic performance, helps schools and youth-serving organizations become more successful, and enhances the well-being of the older adults in the process."

Fellowship for Intentional Community, Netherlands
http://directory.ic.org/intentional_communities_Canada

This lists co-housing experiments in Canada. Senior co-housing is a system of mixed-age residential communities, designed for young and old to live together in mutual support. They are composed of private homes supplemented by shared facilities. The community is planned, owned and managed by the residents – who also share activities which may include cooking, dining, child care, gardening and governance of the community. Common facilities may include a kitchen, dining room, laundry, child care facilities, offices, internet access, guest rooms and recreational features.

Fureai kippu, Japan
These are basic credit units (a kind of local currency) given for helping the elderly. The literal translation is "kindness tickets." Volunteers can accumulate tickets for when they are in need, or arrange for their credits to be paid back by having volunteers visit their relatives who may be living far from them. The services include such things as shopping for the elderly, or taking them to doctor's appointments, etc.

The Good Gym, Britain
http://www.thegoodgym.org/about/

The Good Gym pairs runners with isolated, less-mobile people in their area. Runners jog to the senior's house, deliver something nice, have a brief chat and are on their way again. It helps people get fit by providing a good reason to go for a run and it helps the person being visited by providing them with some friendly human contact and a newspaper or piece of fruit. A low cost initiative that pays good dividends to everyone.

The LIFE Institute, Ryerson University, Canada
https://www.thelifeinstitute.ca/

According to their website, "The LIFE Institute delivers high quality educational programs for older adults covering a wide variety of subjects in the Arts, Humanities, Sciences, Technology and Contemporary Issues. Many of our courses are led by LIFE volunteers."

ITN, United States
http://www.itnamerica.org

On our small island, The Lion's Club provides taxi service one day a week for seniors and folks otherwise unable to get to the stores. ITN is a not-for-profit organization that provides about 50,000 subsidized rides a year to elderly people by bringing volunteers, vehicles and useful computer software together to coordinate such a large scheme. It is partially supported by charities and partially by the elderly, who pay a small annual fee.

Lifeline, North America
www.lifeline.ca

As their advertisement announces, "Philips Lifeline is an easy-to-use personal response service that lets you summon help any time of the day or night – even if you can't speak. All you have to do is press your Personal Help Button, worn on a wristband or pendant, and a trained Personal Response Associate will ensure you get help fast." They say it is a medical alert system that ensures peace of mind. I would add that doesn't mean you shouldn't make sure you have no loose rugs in your home and take other steps to ensure safety.

Mensheds, Australia
http://www.mensheds.org.au

This organization deals with elderly men who often are isolated and marginalized. It addresses their physical, emotional and social health and reaches out to remote regions as well as more populated ones. It especially offers help to men in transitional periods (e.g., redundancy, bereavement, retirement, ill health, relocation, divorce, respite care) in a non-exclusive, non-judgemental way.

OWN, Canada
http://olderwomensnetwork.org

No, not the Oprah Winfrey Network, but the "older women's network," which challenges discrimination on the basis of age, gender, religion, or disability. OWN members offer mutual support and share creative interests and activities. OWN is an educational organization that embraces a feminist perspective in order to empower women to overcome injustices and inequities of gender in the home, the workplace and in society at large. It has also participated in a housing co-op for people on low to medium incomes.

Selfhelp Community Services, Inc., United States
http://www.selfhelp.net/community-services/norcs

Natural Occurring Retirement Communities (NORCs) are communities where long-term, elderly residents wish to remain in their own homes but need support in order to do so. Selfhelp is a group that transforms neighbourhoods, or apartment blocks into retirement communities by providing help with medical needs, transportation, education and recreation. A way of staying in your own home, and getting the neighbourhood support you need to do so.

Tyze, Canada
http://www.tyze.com/

Tyze is a private, Facebook-style online social network that makes it possible for the elderly to coordinate the help they need by building up a network of family, friends and health care providers. It bridges the gap between formal and informal ways of getting assistance.

Naomi Beth Wakan has written over forty books, including *Segues, Late Bloomer: On Writing Later in Life, Compositions: Notes on the written word* and *Book Ends: A year between the covers*. Her book *Haiku – one breath poetry* was an American Library Association selection. Her essays, haiku and tanka have appeared in many magazines and anthologies and have been broadcasted on the CBC. Naomi lives on Gabriola Island with her husband, sculptor Elias Wakan.